THE DISPOSITION OF THE PUBLIC DOMAIN IN OREGON

This is a volume in the
Arno Press collection

THE DEVELOPMENT OF PUBLIC LAND LAW IN THE UNITED STATES

See last pages of this volume for a complete list of titles.

THE DISPOSITION OF THE PUBLIC DOMAIN IN OREGON

[Jerry A. O'Callaghan]

ARNO PRESS
A New York Times Company
New York • 1979

Editorial Supervision: ANDREA HICKS

Reprint Edition 1979 by Arno Press Inc.

Reprinted from a copy in The University of Oregon Library

THE DEVELOPMENT OF PUBLIC LAND LAW IN THE UNITED STATES
ISBN for complete set: 0-405-11363-3
See last pages of this volume for titles.

Manufactured in the United States of America

Library of Congress Cataloging in Publication Data

O'Callaghan, Jerry A
The disposition of the public domain in Oregon.

(The Development of public land law in the United States)
Original t.p. reads: The disposition of the public domain in Oregon, memorandum of the chairman to the Committee on Interior and Insular Affairs, United States Senate, transmitting a dissertation ...
Reprint of the 1930 ed. published by the U. S. Govt. Pub. Print. Off., Washington, D. C.
Based on the author's thesis, Stanford University.
1. Oregon--Public lands. 2. Land settlement--Oregon. I. United States. Congress. Senate. Committee on Interior and Insular Affairs. II. Title. III. Series.
HD243.07024 1979 333.1'09795 78-53563
ISBN 0-405-11382-X

86th Congress, 2d Session } COMMITTEE PRINT

THE DISPOSITION OF THE PUBLIC DOMAIN IN OREGON

MEMORANDUM OF THE CHAIRMAN

TO THE

COMMITTEE ON INTERIOR AND INSULAR AFFAIRS UNITED STATES SENATE

TRANSMITTING A

DISSERTATION SUBMITTED TO THE DEPARTMENT OF HISTORY AND THE COMMITTEE ON GRADUATE STUDY OF STANFORD UNIVERSITY

NOVEMBER 1960

Printed for the use of the Committee on Interior and Insular Affairs

UNITED STATES
GOVERNMENT PRINTING OFFICE
56227 WASHINGTON : 1960

COMMITTEE ON INTERIOR AND INSULAR AFFAIRS

JAMES E. MURRAY, Montana, *Chairman*

CLINTON P. ANDERSON, New Mexico
HENRY M. JACKSON, Washington
JOSEPH C. O'MAHONEY, Wyoming
ALAN BIBLE, Nevada
JOHN A. CARROLL, Colorado
FRANK CHURCH, Idaho
ERNEST GRUENING, Alaska
FRANK E. MOSS, Utah
OREN E. LONG, Hawaii
HALL S. LUSK, Oregon
QUENTIN BURDICK, North Dakota

HENRY DWORSHAK, Idaho
THOMAS H. KUCHEL, California
BARRY GOLDWATER, Arizona
GORDON ALLOTT, Colorado
THOS. E. MARTIN, Iowa
HIRAM L. FONG, Hawaii

RICHARD L. CALLAGHAN, *Staff Director*
STEWART FRENCH, *Chief Counsel*
NELL D. MCSHERRY, *Clerk*

MEMORANDUM OF TRANSMITTAL

U.S. Senate,
Committee on Interior and Insular Affairs,
May 10, 1960.

To the Members of the Committee on Interior and Insular Affairs:

I submit herewith a committee document entitled "The Disposition of the Public Domain in Oregon." Prior to his death, our former colleague, Senator Richard L. Neuberger, called to my attention a dissertation written as a doctoral thesis by Jerry A. O'Callaghan, legislative assistant to Senator Joseph C. O'Mahoney. The abovementioned document incorporates that dissertation as it has been brought up to date by Mr. O'Callaghan.

I believe you will find it a most valuable study of the history of Federal lands in the State of Oregon and a most useful frame of reference in your consideration of land problems existing on the public domain in all States.

James E. Murray, *Chairman.*

LETTER OF SUBMITTAL

U.S. SENATE,
COMMITTEE ON INTERIOR AND INSULAR AFFAIRS,
December 2, 1959.

Hon. JAMES E. MURRAY,
Chairman, Committee on Interior and Insular Affairs,
U.S. Senate, Washington, D.C.

DEAR SENATOR MURRAY: Recently I had the opportunity of reviewing "Disposition of the Public Domain in Oregon," which I am enclosing. It is Jerry O'Callaghan's (legislative assistant to Senator O'Mahoney) doctoral dissertation at Stanford submitted in 1951, and I consider it an excellent job.

It seems to me that a thesis such as this would be a valuable thing to have printed as a committee print so that it could be used in connection with public-land legislation. In fact, I am inclined to think that our committee might well sponsor the publication of a similar document for each of the public-land States.

I would like to ask you to publish Jerry O'Callaghan's thesis this fall. May I suggest that he handle the project but that he may want to call on Jim Gamble to help update the action taken on the Klamath Reservation and Bob Wolf to help footnote the action of the 83d Congress on the controverted O. & C. lands. With these two revisions and such editorial adjustments as Jerry might wish to make, the thesis would be completely up to date.

If you agree to this and if you desire, I will glad be to prepare an introduction for the print.

With best wishes, I am,

Sincerely,

Dick Neuberger,
RICHARD L. NEUBERGER,
U.S. Senator.

THE DISPOSITION OF THE PUBLIC DOMAIN IN OREGON

BY

JERRY A. O'CALLAGHAN

PREFACE

Anyone familiar with the genre will immediately recognize this study for what it is—a doctoral dissertation. It has been revised, by editorial excision of words found surplus when read 9 years after their writing and use of later statistics where appropriate as well as noting important developments since 1950. These intervening years have been active ones which have included teaching at Stanford University, where the dissertation was written, and at the University of Wyoming; editing the oil pages of the Casper Tribune-Herald at Casper, Wyo., long the exploration center of the Rocky Mountain oil province; and serving nearly 4 years as legislative assistant to Senator Joseph C. O'Mahoney, whose many responsibilities in the Senate have, in late years, included the chairmanship of the Public Lands Subcommittee of the Committee on Interior and Insular Affairs. These years and these positions have all contributed a greater knowledge of the public lands but have precluded any further pursuit of their disposition in Oregon.

If time and circumstance had permitted, I should have preferred to investigate further the story of homesteading in Oregon. The first investigation was necessarily confined to official documents and the files of the Oregonian. Beyond the statistical, there is a surprising lack of material in these sources. Undoubtedly, there is in the files of country newspapers and the scattered letters and private papers a wealth of material yet to be collected and assayed with respect to homesteading in Oregon. I have chosen, however, to publish in its present form this story of "The Disposition of the Public Domain in Oregon" in the belief that a contribution can be made at this time.

This is a modest effort, yet there are many to whom I am greatly indebted for encouragement, advice, and information. Those to whom public acknowledgement would be most fitting include: Senator Joseph C. O'Mahoney, who has given me opportunity as his legislative assistant to learn much about many affairs including the public lands; Richard Callaghan, staff director, Senate Committee on Interior and Insular Affairs, and Stewart French, its chief counsel; E. D. Eaton, Robert Wolf, James Gamble, members of its professional staff, and Harold Symes, its printing editorial assistant; E. E. Robinson, chairman emeritus, department of history, Stanford University; and the late Dan E. Clark, onetime chairman, department of history, University of Oregon.

I have many regrets about the untimely death of Senator Richard L. Neuberger of Oregon. A minor one is that Senator Neuberger, whose suggestion it was that this work be printed by the Committee on Interior and Insular Affairs, cannot be the author of the preface which he indicated he desired to write for it.

Wives of scholars are universally called upon, it seems, to bear a large share of the responsibilities of scholarship. Florence Sheehan O'Callaghan has responded in this instance with the intelligence, wit, and affection which are characteristic of her in all endeavors.

JERRY A. O'CALLAGHAN.

WASHINGTON, D.C., *May 10, 1960.*

CONTENTS

	Page
Introduction:	
Physiography of Oregon	1
Statistics on disposition in Oregon	2
Chapter I. The early settlement of Oregon, 1840–60:	
"Oregon Fever"	3
Character of pioneers	5
Boundary settlement	5
Provisional government	7
Its land legislation	8
Chapter II. Later settlement of Oregon, 1860–1910:	
Settlement of eastern Oregon	11
Mining and the cattle industry	12
Railroad construction	13
Land promotion by the railroads	14
Homesteads in eastern Oregon	16
Irrigation and reclamation	17
Population increase	18
Chapter III. Extinguishing the Indian title:	
Delayed extinguishment	21
Joel Palmer's negotiations	23
Unratified treaties and the Yakima war	24
Congressional responsibility	25
Encroachment upon Indian land	26
Klamath termination	27
Chapter IV. The Donation Land Act:	
The Linn bills	31
Passage of the Donation Act	32
Congressional debate	33
The Donation Act and the Hudson's Bay Co	33
Importance of the act	34
Chapter V. The Oregon & California grant:	
Authorization in 1866	37
The designation struggle	38
Changes in congressional attitudes	39
The "actual settler" clause	39
Sale of the grant lands	41
Southern Pacific closure	42
Authorization for recovery suit	43
Before the Supreme Court	44
The Ferris-Chamberlain Act	45
Chapter VI. The wagon road grants:	
Wagon road grants in Mississippi Valley	49
Five military wagon roads in Oregon	50
Oregon Central Military Wagon Road	50
The Willamette Valley and Cascade Mountain Wagon Road Co	52
The Dalles Military Wagon Road	54
The Corvallis and Yaquina Bay Wagon Road	55
The Coos Bay Wagon Road	55
Forfeiture suits	56
Oregon Central grant and the Klamath Indians	58
Chapter VII. Grant to the State of Oregon:	
State lands in the timber boom	61
Land provisions of the admission act	63
School lands	64
The internal improvement grant	66
The university grant	66
The agricultural college grant	67
Swamp lands	67
Minor grants	70

	Page
Chapter VIII. The disposition of timber lands:	
Early lack of value	71
Private ownership of timber	72
The commuted homestead	74
The Timber and Stone Act	74
Timberland locators	75
The Northern Pacific grant and the Forest Lieu Act	78
The Southern Pacific as timber owner	80
Present ownership pattern	82
Chapter IX. Land fraud in the timber:	
Stephen A. Douglas Puter and the 11–7 case	86
Francis J. Heney as special prosecutor	88
Trial of Senator Mitchell	89
Blue Mountain Reserve conspiracy	92
Trials of Congressman Williamson	93
Acquittals of Binger Hermann	94
Dismissal of numerous indictments	94
Chapter X. The Homestead Act and after:	
Twentieth century homesteading	97
Original and final entry	98
Cash sales	99
Railroad grants	100
Land ownership pattern	101
Summary	103
Appendix	107
Bibliography	109

INTRODUCTION

Physiographers divide Oregon into eight physiographic provinces: the Coast province, the Willamette Valley province, the Cascade plateau, the Klamath province, the Snake River plains, the Southeastern Lake province, the Blue-Wallowa Mountain province, and the Columbia-Deschutes province.[1] In general designation Oregon is more simply divided into eastern and western Oregon, separated by the Cascade Range. It is easy to think that the Cascades divide Oregon equally into an eastern and western half. Actually eastern Oregon is the larger as the Cascades leave western Oregon as one-quarter and eastern Oregon as three-quarters of the State.

Western Oregon was the first settled and is the most populous. Its scenery and climate have given Oregon its reputation as the Webfoot State. A heavy rainfall in western Oregon fosters an evergreen forest of Douglas fir and the dominant color is green. Rainfall is heaviest on the coast, where at certain points it reaches 140 inches annually. Western Oregon is a mountainous forested mass with arable river valleys, notably the Willamette, between ranges. The Coast Range and the Cascades extend parallel to the coastline; between the two ranges are connecting east-west spurs. Three important river valleys in western Oregon support the heaviest population of the State. The largest and most populous is the Willamette Valley. It takes its name from a main tributary of the Columbia and extends from Eugene, where the river emerges from the Cascade foothills, to the Columbia north of Portland. It is a long valley of fertile farmland, rolling hills, and temperate climate. The Willamette Valley was the goal of the first American migrations to the Northwest. Portland, the only metropolitan area of the State, is its great trading city.

The other river valleys are the Umpqua, with Roseburg as its main city, and the Rogue, with Medford and Grants Pass as its chief trading centers. Both are interior valleys, as the Coast Range blocks their extension to the Pacific. Western Oregon has a marine climate, which means heavy rainfall with equable temperatures.

In direct contrast are the high plains and plateaus of eastern Oregon. The land east of the Cascades, which is volcanic in origin, is a land more brown than green, an arid and semiarid land, with irrigation an absolute necessity, except for grain, for the production of staple crops. Average rainfall is as low as 9 inches on the Steens Mountains in southeastern Oregon. Eastern Oregon is a land of long vistas, mountain ranges rising from a volcanic plateau, and sparse population. Some of the valleys are irrigated and highly productive, but subject to late and early frosts. There are several distinct stands of ponderosa pine.

[1] Warren D. Smith, "Physical and Economic Geography of Oregon," Commonwealth Review, VI (1924), p. 82; map, p. 78.

Oregon is not a populous State. In 1940 it averaged 11.3 persons per square mile. In 1950, with a 412,000 increase in population, it averaged 15.6 per square mile. By 1950 Oregon's population was 1,521,341.[2] In 1960 the census takers reported 1,757,691 Oregonians in the preliminary release. At this figure the number per square mile rose handily to 18.3 Eastern Oregon claimed 263,084 and western the remaining 1,494,607 persons.

The transportation network converges on Portland, on the Willamette River 10 miles above its confluence with the Columbia River, making it the one metropolitan area (Multnomah County's population is 468,571) in the State.

The rivers of Oregon give Portland its predominant position in transportation. Except for the Columbia, the important rivers flow to the north. The railways followed in a general way the configuration given by the rivers. The main line Southern Pacific enters Portland via the Willamette Valley. The Union Pacific and the Spokane, Portland & Seattle enter Portland by way of the natural gorge which the Columbia River has torn through the Cascade Range. Portland is, as Glenn Chesney Quiett has written in "They Built the West," the city that gravity built.

The land area of the State of Oregon is 61,664,000 acres.[3] In 1850, except for a vague Indian title, the ownership was vested in the U.S. Government. In the hundred years between 1850 and 1950, the Federal Government has sold or granted to individuals, companies and the State of Oregon, 29,569,403 acres.[4] This is approximately one-half the land in Oregon and is by all odds the most immediately valuable. It is the land of the arable valleys and the best timberland. This land was turned over to private persons (which includes companies) with the view that the general interest of the Government and the society it represented could best be served by transferring the public lands through gift and sale to individuals for development by those individuals.

In the pages which follow, the settlement of Oregon, particularly the later settlement, which has never been fully treated, will be outlined as a prelude to extended discussion of the land laws, operation of which was particularly applicable to Oregon.

Disposition of the public domain in Oregon

[In acres]

Homestead	11, 097, 982	Railroad grants	1, 588, 532
Sales	6, 455, 551	Miscellaneous	992, 921
Grant to State	4, 329, 445		
Donation claims	2, 614, 082	Total	29, 569, 403
Wagon road grants	2, 490, 890		

NOTE.—These totals have been computed from statistics in "Senate Documents," 58th Cong., 3d sess., No. 189, and from a recapitulation of Oregon figures furnished by the Bureau of Land Management.

[2] Bureau of the Census, 17th Census, Vol. I, Number of Inhabitants. The 1960 figures are furnished by the Bureau of the Census from its preliminary reports.

[3] Bureau of the Census, Statistical Abstract of the United States, 1950 (Washington, 1950), p. 162.

[4] There is no published total for Oregon disposition. This total was constructed from statistics in the last compendium of public land statistics, "The Report of the Public Lands Commission" (1905), which was printed in "Senate Documents," 58th Cong., 3d sess., No. 189; and from unpublished statistics furnished by the Bureau of Land Management.

CHAPTER I

THE EARLY SETTLEMENT OF OREGON, 1840–60

"OREGON FEVER"

Early in the 1840's an "Oregon fever" swept over the United States. Its ravages, if such they may be called, descended heavily on the upper Mississippi Valley. Agriculture was still languishing from the panic of 1837; transportation did not favor the trans-Appalachian farmer; fertile land was available, but the cheapest cost the Government minimum of $1.25 per acre; large tracts were going into speculative holdings; and the undrained swamps and uncleared forests were debilitating.

Into the Mississippi Valley filtered word of a wondrous Willamette Valley in a far corner of the continent where the acres were fertile and the climate healthful, and where, furthermore, land was waiting to be saved for the United States. Publicists such as Hall J. Kelley made the promotion of Oregon a lifework. In 1838, as part of the diplomatic contest for Oregon, a Missouri Senator, Lewis Linn, introduced a bill providing extension of American Government to Oregon and offering land for those who would emigrate. Western Representatives and Senators began to bombard their followers with speeches, letters, and information about Oregon. Letters from Oregonians were published in the newspapers of their old hometowns and then republished. Peter H. Burnett, who went to Oregon in 1843, wrote a letter to Missouri which was published in 30 newspapers.[1]

Men in public position in the West premeditatedly fostered agitation for Oregon. On that land-hungry frontier, talk of fertile land to be won from Great Britain struck a responsive chord. Editors added their exhortations. Estimates of emigration were made on the basis of those who talked about moving. Settlers already in Oregon well knew the rise in value of their holdings that an increase in population would bring and their letters went home to add to the fever.

The Linn bills, with their provision for a land grant, were an annual appearance in Congress. Their land provisions varied from 640 acres to 1,000 acres as a reward to Americans who would emigrate to Oregon to contest its possession with Great Britain.[2] One bill's terms would have granted 640 acres with an additional 160 acres for each child in a family. Peter H. Burnett, first Governor of California, was working off an indebtedness in Missouri when this bill was under consideration. He estimated that a move to Oregon would net him 1,600 acres. He gives this as his principal motive in removing with the migration of 1843.[3]

[1] This analysis of "Oregon Fever" is largely based on Melvin Clay Jacobs, "Winning Oregon: A Study of an Expansionist Movement" (Caldwell, Idaho, 1938), pp. 43–51.
[2] See ch. IV.
[3] Peter H. Burnett, "Recollections and Opinions of an Old Pioneer" (New York, 1880), pp. 97–98.

When one of these bills passed the Senate in 1843, it was taken in the West as a binding promise to reward emigration to Oregon with land. Men sold their farms in the Mississippi Valley for a "song without a tune" to purchase an outfit to join the 2,500-mile trek. Starting slowly in 1840, the "Oregon fever" and the consequent migration rolled to a climax in 1848 when it gave way to another fever—for California gold, though California had shared in the "Oregon fever" even before the discovery of gold.

In 1840, the American population in Oregon was estimated as 137, plus 63 French-Canadians not connected with the Hudson's Bay Co.[4] In 1850, in the first U.S. census to cover Oregon, there were 13,294. Overland emigration started slowly. In 1841, there were 75 people; in 1843, there were 111.[5] The first considerable migration was that of 1843. It added 875 people, including 295 men over 16. This migration was numerically surpassed by later ones, but it was a decisive increment in Oregon's American settlement. In May of 1843, a half year before the arrival of that year's migration, the tentative steps to provisional government had carried by an uncomfortably small margin; the deciding votes had come from two French-Canadians friendly to the Americans.[6] The emigration of 1843 ended for all time the narrow margin of American sentiment. The migration of 1844 added 1,400 and that of 1845, 3,000. In 1846, 1,500 to 1,700 came and in 1847, 3,000 to 4,000.[7]

The birthplace of the 52 men who voted for a provisional government at Champoeg in May 1843 is a clue to the source of the emigration to Oregon. Ten of the fifty-two had been born in New York; five in England; four each in Connecticut and Pennsylvania; three each in New Hampshire and Ohio; two each in Vermont, Canada, and Scotland; one each in Alabama, the District of Columbia, Indiana, Ireland, Kentucky, Maine, Massachusetts, North Carolina, and Virginia; and five were unspecified.[8]

In 1850, when the population numbered 13,000, the overwhelming percentage had emigrated from the Mississippi Valley. Missouri led all States in the numbers contributed; a significantly large number of these were children born in the transition from older homes farther to the east. The States most heavily represented in the 1850 population were Iowa, Missouri, Illinois, Indiana, Tennessee, Kentucky, Ohio, New York, Pennsylvania, and Virginia.[9] All save three were States of the Ohio or upper Mississippi Valley, a fact noted by Albert J. Beveridge in his monumental biography of Abraham Lincoln in which he described the exodus from Illinois as Lincoln saw it.

> The fact that immense areas of fertile land and beautiful country in Illinois were still vacant mattered not at all to these searchers for the unknown and fabulous.[10]

---

[4] Frederick V. Holman, "A Brief History of the Oregon Provisional Government and What Caused Its Formation," Quarterly of the Oregon Historical Society, XIII (1912), 105. (Note: For convenience the "Quarterly of the Oregon Historical Society," later the "Oregon Historical Quarterly," will be cited O.H.Q."

[5] Jacobs, "Winning Oregon," 47 n.

[6] Holman, loc. cit., p. 113.

[7] Ibid., p. 132.

[8] Ibid., p. 115.

[9] Jesse Douglas, "Origins of the Population of Oregon in 1850," Pacific Northwest Quarterly, XLI (1950), 105.

[10] Albert J. Beveridge, "Abraham Lincoln, 1809–58" (Boston, 1928), II, 167–68.

CHARACTER OF PIONEERS

Oregon was not settled by the squatters typical of the frontier advance into the Mississippi Valley. Although the men and women coming to Oregon came to better themselves, they were not without substance and standing in their home communities. The costs of migration to Oregon effectively barred a large number who might otherwise have answered the call of free land,[11] land which could be owned by possession and cultivation. The men who went to Oregon were men who had farms to sell in the Mississippi Valley. Others might be taken into the caravans if they were well recommended; such were usually employed in the responsible job of tending the cattle.[12]

James Clymer, returning from a trip to Oregon and California in 1846, marked it down as—

> * * * strange that so many of all kinds and classes of people should sell comfortable homes * * * pack and start across such an immense barren waste, to settle in some new place, of which they have, at most, uncertain information.[13]

A Missouri newspaper in 1843, commenting on the caliber of men in the migration of 1843, said—

> There are in the expedition a number of citizens of inestimable value to any community * * * men of fine intelligence and vigorous and intrepid character * * *.[14]

An Iowa newspaper described the men preparing for the Oregon trek in 1845 as—

> * * * generally men of respectability and good standing * * * and they carry with them not only necessities but many luxuries of life.[15]

Another side to the character of Oregon pioneers has been described by Frederick Merk. In explaining the pugnacity of Oregon settlers regarding Great Britain and the Hudson's Bay Co., he noted that they came from the Missouri border, "* * * communities notorious for turbulence and readiness for self-help * * *." Oregon settlers were "Southern uplanders, contentious, ignorant, and suspicious * * *."[16] In these unflattering terms, Merk is characterizing a faction, which, whatever its numbers, was vociferous in its antagonism to Britain and the Hudson's Bay Co., a faction which recognized no British equity in Oregon and was furious at the protection of property accorded the Hudson's Bay Co. in the treaty of 1846.

BOUNDARY SETTLEMENT

Oregon settlers in the Willamette Valley felt and acted as if they had saved Oregon from the British. In their minds the title of the Oregon country belonged exclusively to the United States. Echoes of this extreme attitude sounded through the legislative halls. In fact, such sentiments may have been instigated by western spokesmen themselves.[17] Edward A. Hannegan, Indiana Senator, obliged the West on February 10, 1846, with a resolution to bind the executive

[11] Jacobs, "Winning Oregon," p. 52.
[12] Ibid., p. 53.
[13] Oregon Spectator, Apr. 29, 1847, cited in Jacobs, "Winning Oregon," p. 53.
[14] Ibid., p. 54.
[15] Ibid., p. 55.
[16] Frederick Merk, "Oregon Pioneers and the Boundary," "American Historical Review," XXIX (1923–24), 693.
[17] Jacobs, "Winning Oregon," pp. 160–61.

branch in any negotiation with Great Britain. The Hannegan resolution asserted that the whole of Oregon to 54 degrees 40 minutes latitude was part and parcel of the United States and no power existed to transfer it.[18] Western expansionists shied from negotiation with Great Britain. They had never forgiven Daniel Webster, Tyler's Secretary of State, for his surrender of "American" territory in the Webster-Ashburton Treaty of 1842.

The West was antagonistic to the Tyler administration for its cool attitude to expansion. Western spokesmen became vocal when the Webster-Ashburton Treaty did not include a settlement of the Oregon boundary. Westerners called down an anathema upon Webster for his "betrayal" in fixing the Maine boundary. One western editor even feared that Webster might sell the whole of the Oregon country in any negotiation with Britain.[19]

Webster was probably not going to sell Oregon, but he was decidedly unenthusiastic about its acquisition. His thoughts about the Pacific coast went to harbors for Yankee ships, not farms for the turbulent, ambitious agrarians of the West. He and Tyler had their own plan for expansion.[20] They conceived a Mexican cession of Texas and northern California to include the great bay at San Francisco. Great Britain was to be permitted the Columbia for a southern boundary. Texas was to be annexed for the South and the San Francisco Harbor for the Northeast. The West was not in this reckoning. It wanted both California and all of Oregon.

James K. Polk entered the White House in March 1845, prepared to grant the West its desires. He had been elected in 1844 with "reannexation of Texas" and "reoccupation of Oregon" as the trumpet call of his campaign. At the beginning of his administration, an adroitly worded resolution authorizing abrogation of the joint occupation passed House and Senate.[21]

The Democratic demand in 1844 had been "Fifty-four Forty or Fight." This extreme demand was based upon Spanish claims and the Monroe Doctrine. It was not to be easily enforced against Great Britain. The diplomatic maneuverings and the changes in political weather, both in the United States and in Great Britain, which allowed the rational extension of the 49th parallel as the boundary from the Rocky Mountains to the Strait of Juan de Fuca, need not be recounted here.[22] A treaty, ratified June 15, 1846, was arranged with Great Britain with prior Senate approval. It was an equitable solution, even if a western editor would write:

> Withered be the hand that dismembers Oregon, and palsied the tongue that consents to an act so treasonable, foul, and unnatural.[23]

Actually, the United States did very well. Imminence of American settlement, rather than actual settlement, north of the Columbia River, prompted a British willingness to compromise on the 49th parallel.

American settlement did not directly save Oregon. The Willamette Valley, where the Americans had settled, had never been demanded

18 The Congressional Globe, 29th Cong., 1st sess., p. 351.
19 Jacobs, "Winning Oregon," pp. 126–28.
20 Ibid., pp. 131–32.
21 The Congressional Globe, 29th Cong., 1st sess., pp. 692, 717.
22 There is an admirable summary in Frederick Jackson Turner, "The United States 1830–50: The Nation and Its Sections" (New York, 1935), pp. 544–545, 549, 551–554.
23 Quoted in Thomas A. Bailey, "The Diplomatic History of the American People," third edition (New York, 1946), p. 244.

by the British. By 1846, the choice lands in the valley were settled and Americans were poised to cross the Columbia. With this threat, and a decline in the fur trade, the Hudson's Bay Co. leadership signified that the Columbia would no longer be the vital boundary it once had seemed.[24] The Hudson's Bay was the paramount British interest and, with its interest declining, the British Government could accept another boundary.

Settlement in the Willamette Valley was not by chance. This long valley, alternating meadow and woodland, was an agrarian magnet in the expanse of heavy forest which covered western Oregon from the crest of the Cascades to the Pacific. Fertility of soil and certainty that its title would go to the United States prompted its American settlement.[25] Not until 1846, when the most desirable of the Willamette Valley land had been staked out, did American settlers drift north of the Columbia River to begin encroachment upon the Hudson's Bay holdings.[26]

PROVISIONAL GOVERNMENT

Neither Great Britain nor the United States had exercised any real power in the Oregon country. Great Britain, in 1821, had delegated substantial power to the Hudson's Bay Co. to preserve law and order among British citizens. The American Government did not make any arrangements. In a way it was not necessary. American settlers with their own penchant for local self-government were quick enough to establish their own government. In 1841, when there were only 250 people in the valley, there were men urging a local government. The death of the valley's most prosperous citizen in February 1841 emphasized a need for government in some form. Ewing Young had died without a will and apparently without heirs. In an organized community, his estate would have escheated to the State but in the Oregon country his death demonstrated the need for local government in some form.

Sentiment for local government centered at the start in the missionary circles, whose dominating figure was the Reverend Jason Lee. John McLoughlin, chief factor of the Hudson's Bay Co., was not favorably disposed to early attempts at local government.[27] He suspected quite correctly that its organizers were unfriendly to him and his company. The sentiment for government remained dormant until February and March of 1843 when the first and second Wolf meetings were held. These meetings had as their result another meeting of valley settlers at Champoeg, May 2, 1843. The famous Champoeg meeting, where the vote was in favor of local government, completed a rudimentary organization. It had no powers of taxation and was much more an expression of sentiment for government than an effective government. But it suited local needs.

A prime interest in establishing government was promotion of the security of land claims. In fact, this may have been the primary, though unexpressed, aim of the organizers. It is no disparagement to say that whatever other motives may have led Americans to Oregon, the most immediate was farmland, to be purchased by

[24] Merk, loc. cit., pp. 695–696.
[25] Merk, loc. cit., p. 687.
[26] Ibid., p. 687.
[27] Holman, loc. cit., p. 104.

improvement and development, not cash. And it is a truism, of course, that there are no property values without government.

ITS LAND LEGISLATION

By 1843, the missionary group was not as eager for government. Jason Lee had doubts about its ability to dominate. The arrival of the migration of 1843, in the fall of that year, was to prove him right. In the land law passed by the legislative committee in 1843, a definite inducement was included to attract missionary support.[28] It allowed a claim of 640 acres for an individual in square or oblong shape. For the missionary stations, however, it provided a claim 6 miles square.

Arrival of the migration of 1843 changed entirely the complexion of Oregon politics. American sentiment was now in overwhelming preponderance. Within the American community, the missionary influence was submerged. The land law of 1843 did not commend itself to the new arrivals. The leaders objected to it as "a missionary arrangement to secure the most valuable farming land * * *." [29] The missionaries no longer had to be curried and the provision for a township claim was dropped in the land law of 1844 at the same time the conditions for holding a claim were made more explicit. Claims were restricted to men over age 18, unless they were married. Improvement had to be made and occupancy, either in person or by a tenant, was required to deter speculation.[30]

A stronger provisional government came into being in 1845 with enactment of an organic law. In August of that year, McLoughlin and the Hudson's Bay Co. joined the provisional government insofar as it did not conflict with their British citizenship. From its inception, the provisional government had been organized to serve only until the United States could extend itself to Oregon. Because the United States made no provision for local government, the provisional government served 3 years when Oregon was nominally under the jurisdiction of the United States. Territorial government was not instituted until March 3, 1849, although Oregon had become a possession on June 15, 1846.

Provisional land claims were not confirmed by the Federal Government in the Oregon Territorial Act of 1848. While it confirmed the laws of the provisional government not inconsistent with Federal law or the Constitution, on the all-important subject of landownership it annulled the land legislation of the provisional government without making any arrangement to grant or sell public lands in Oregon.[31]

Oregon settlers were convinced that they had a legal right to their land, not only because of the provisional law, but because the lands, in their opinions, had been promised by Senate passage of the 1843 Linn bill and public men had encouraged Oregon migration. An extreme Oregon opinion was set forth in the Oregon Spectator, by M. M. McCarver, a leader in the provisional government. He indicated not only the right but the route of appeal:

> Our title is already valid to the full amount * * * although the bill has not yet passed; and that right is in each individual and cannot be diminished without his individual consent. Although we may not be able in organized courts of

[28] LaFayette Grover, "The Archives of Oregon: including the Journals, Governor's Messages, and Public Papers of Oregon (Salem, 1853), p. 35.
[29] Burnett, "Recollections and Opinions of an Old Pioneer," p. 204.
[30] Ibid., pp. 201-202.
[31] Stat., IX, 329.

civil jurisprudence to perfect our title at present, yet there is a higher court * * * a court to which the highest authorities of the nation must bow with submission, we mean that high court of chancery, the sovereign people * * *.[32]

This view was confirmed in 1847 by Lt. Neil Howison, an official visitor to Oregon. In his report to his naval superiors he predicted that Oregon settlers would not pay $1.25 per acre for their land. They did not have the money and they were firmly convinced that the land was theirs without payment.[33]

The results of the provisional government's land legislation were inconclusive. After Oregon's title passed to the United States, only the Federal Government could dispose of public lands or confirm existing claims. Indirectly the provisional claims were confirmed with the passage of the Donation Land Act in 1850.

---

[32] Oregon Spectator, Sept. 3, 1846.

[33] "House Miscellaneous Documents," 30th Cong., 1st sess., No. 29, p. 32.

CHAPTER II

LATER SETTLEMENT OF OREGON, 1860–1910

SETTLEMENT OF EASTERN OREGON

The first emigrants to Oregon passed by the eastern Oregon country. Their eyes were fixed on the often described fertile acres of the Willamette Valley. Such a practical visionary as Marcus Whitman realized the possibilities, with irrigation, of this "upper country," but the mass of Americans migrating to Oregon passed to the valleys of western Oregon with few, if any, thoughts of homebuilding on the plateaus and highlands of eastern Oregon.

In typical American fashion, a generation later, the sons of the first generation of American settlers in the Willamette Valley had turned their eyes eastward and were stirred by thoughts of the high country which lay "beyond the ranges." In the 1880's "half the young men of the Willamette Valley," one writer observed, "were burning to try their fortunes" east of the mountains.[1] By the 1900's the donation land claims in the Willamette Valley had largely passed from the hands of the original owners or their descendants. T. W. Davenport, a State senator and onetime State land agent, numbered among the reasons the attraction of cattle ranching in eastern Oregon, which drew the young men away from the "old homestead" in the valley.[2]

The settlement of western Oregon was far from complete in the 1850's, but the main outline of development was well marked. Further increase in population would place people on the foothill lands and add to the growth of towns already started.

The early settlement of eastern Oregon is difficult to chronicle. Topography has dictated scattered settlement. Eastern Oregon was populated by a backthrust of settlement from Western Oregon implemented by a "new" immigration promoted by the railroads. The choice valley lands of western Oregon went to the firstcomers of the forties and fifties. As population increased and a new generation came to adulthood in the Willamette Valley, the American urge to get a new start in a new land began to attract families from western Oregon.

The Northern Pacific, after much trial and tribulation, was completed to Portland in 1883. Henry Villard, the German-born journalist turned railroad magnate, fully realized the elementary fact that the Northwest would need increasing increments of population to exploit its resources and furnish freight for his Northern Pacific and Oregon & California Railroad. He systematically began a campaign, in 1874, to induce immigration to the Pacific Northwest. Both the Northern Pacific and Oregon & California had land grants to sell, but Villard's objective was greater than the sale of these grants.

[1] Wallis Nash, "Two Years in Oregon" (New York, 1882), p. 231.
[2] T. W. Davenport, "An Object Lesson in Paternalism," O.H.Q., IV (1903), 51.

The early farmers of the Mississippi Valley who had come to Oregon had come the long 2,500 miles from the Missouri River by ox train. The new immigrant came by "the iron horse," shepherded by railroad company agents. Immigrant trains, with special rates for passengers and household goods, were run West. In these "colonist" trains the family cooking was done in the traveling cars with immigrants furnishing their own food and bedding.

MINING AND THE CATTLE INDUSTRY

Before the settlers bent on farming arrived, mining set the cadence of the American advance into the inland empire. Gold was discovered at Colville, Washington Territory, in 1855. In 1858, the Fraser River attracted a big mining population. There were gold rushes to the Cariboo and Kootenai fields in British Columbia in the early 1860's. Strikes on the Clearwater in present Idaho and on the John Day and Powder Rivers in Oregon and the famous rushes in western Montana all prompted the occupation of the pastoral lands in eastern Oregon.[3]

The California gold rush had made western Oregon cattle a valuable commodity. And the mining activity in the Inland Empire, as the Columbia plateau has come to be called, was to do the same for eastern Oregon. The range cattle industry suffered the same boom-and-bust cycle in eastern Oregon as on the Great Plains.[4] The 1860's were profitable cattle years. The mines of Idaho and western Montana were in full blast and the supply of cattle was limited. Cattle were introduced into northeastern Oregon in 1861 and into the Powder River, John Day, and Owyhee Valleys shortly thereafter. Later in the decade settlement began in Harney County. The margins of Klamath and Goose Lakes, near the California boundary, were settled as cattle country in 1870; at the same time, Wasco County in north-central Oregon was settled with people from the Willamette Valley.[5] The natural increase in the cattle herds depressed the price in the mid-1870's.

County names give a clue to settlement dates. Polk, Benton, Linn, Douglas—so run the county names of western Oregon, honoring the public men of the 1840's and 1850's. Grant, Sherman, and Union are county names in eastern Oregon honoring men and sentiment of the 1860's. Creation of counties in eastern Oregon is not conclusive indication of full settlement. The need for local government preceded establishment of towns. Counties were created as a convenience for early settlers, who otherwise might have had to travel 250 miles to a county seat.[6]

Cattlemen were not alone in their occupation of this "high country." Sheepmen and wheat farmers were close behind. By 1876, wheat was shown to be suitable for the arable hill lands of eastern Oregon,[7] particularly in the country just south of the Columbia River. When the transcontinental connections were made in 1883–84, the railroads began to pour a new stream of homeseekers and laborers into Oregon. This stream went both to western and eastern Oregon, but eastern Oregon offered certain advantages to newcomers, particularly those

[3] James Orin Oliphant, "The Range Cattle Industry in the Oregon Country to 1890" (unpublished doctoral dissertation in Harvard University Library), pp. 104, 126.
[4] Oliphant, "The Range Cattle Industry in the Oregon Country to 1890," pp. 92, 126–127.
[5] Ibid., p. 104.
[6] Charles Henry Carey, "History of Oregon" (Chicago, 1922), p. 767.
[7] The Oregonian, Mar. 20, 1876; editorial, Apr. 26, 1876.

with little cash who wanted land cheap. By the 1870's, western Oregon was an "old" part of the Nation. It had been settled for a generation. In the latter decades of the 19th century, cheap Government land for farming or ranching could be found in eastern Oregon. As an Oregonian editorial pointed out in 1871, many newcomers were disappointed in coming to western Oregon because they thought they were coming to a new country but which was, in fact, as "old as Minnesota or Kansas." [8] The available land in western Oregon in the 1870's needed clearing to make it arable.

In eastern Oregon the encroachment of sheep and wheat steadily compressed the effective range cattle industry. The cattlemen, of course, opposed this drift; but in the arable counties, as in the northeast, they could not stem the tide, aided as it was by the railroads.[9] In central Oregon, the cattle industry had an ally. The great 800,000 acre grant of the Willamette Valley and Cascade Mountain Wagon Road Co. was owned by a California land company which did not sell its holdings until 1910.[10] Settlers and would be settlers were touched in a sensitive spot—dread of land monopoly—but the cattlemen were glad to lease land from the company which held it off the settlement market.

The range cattle industry was passing by 1890 into a new age. Overstocking, encroachment of homesteading, and competition forced a withdrawal, particularly after 1900, into southeastern Oregon, the present stronghold. There, natural conditions, large blocks of land acquired through swampland sales,[11] and military wagon grant sales held down the partitioning inherent in homesteading.[12]

RAILROAD CONSTRUCTION

The railroad net which Oregon acquired in the 1880's, as has been indicated, played a decisive role in the reduction of the eastern Oregon wilderness. This is not the place to narrate in detail the long, even desperate, struggle of Oregon to acquire its greatly needed connections to the East.

The Southern Pacific, Union Pacific, and Northern Pacific lines formed the basic structure of Oregon's rail network. After this spasm, major railroad construction relaxed. For all this pioneer railroad building, there were great parts of Oregon, particularly the interior of eastern Oregon, without rail transportation. This was remedied, in part, early in the 20th century by the rivalry of two railroad giants, almost the last of their kind. James J. Hill built his Great Northern to Puget Sound in 1893. E. H. Harriman became an Oregon railroad figure through his control of the Union Pacific and later the Southern Pacific.

Their rivalry in Oregon was, in part, an economic waste, but it opened the central Oregon country, centering around Bend, to 20th century settlement. Hill arrived in Oregon when his North Bank Railroad—now the Spokane, Portland, & Seattle—was completed to Portland in 1908. Hill challenged the Harriman domination of Oregon rail transportation by sending his construction battalions across the Columbia into the Deschutes Canyon to begin building to

[8] The Oregonian, May 13, 1871.
[9] Oliphant, "The Range Cattle Industry in the Oregon Country to 1890," p. 182.
[10] The same situation applied to the other eastern Oregon wagon road grants. They are treated in ch. VI.
[11] The swamplands are treated in ch. VII.
[12] Dexter K. Strong, "Beef Cattle Industry in Oregon, 1890–1938," O.H.Q., XLI (1940), 261.

Bend, 165 miles to the south. Harriman opposed the Oregon Trunk Railway construction with a legal battle and a parallel grade. The contest reached an impasse at Metolius, and the two giants compromised. Hill built into Bend, arriving in 1911, and the Harriman lines used his trackage between Metolius and Bend.

LAND PROMOTION BY THE RAILROADS

All these railroads had more than a casual interest in the settlement of Oregon. The Pacific railroads were a decisive factor, if not the decisive factor, in the final reduction of unsettled American land. The thousands who climbed off the railroad cars after the trip across the continent were not all there by happy chance. Henry Villard, who ultimately guided the affairs of two railroads and one steamship company, systematically cultivated emigration. He established in 1874 an emigration bureau for the Oregon & California Railroad. It had an office in Portland and Boston. New England farmers and northern Europeans were Villard's favorities for the new immigration.[13]

Besides the Boston office, the Oregon & California opened offices in Topeka and Omaha to direct immigration to the Northwest. These efforts had their effect in diverting people from California, as one newspaper was to complain. Villard's agents were in New York, Boston, and the great ports of Europe distributing "literature" and arranging details of transportation. In mid-America the agents were at junction points like Topeka and Omaha to brace the fainthearted and to convince the California bound that their true destiny was in Oregon and the Northwest.

> It was this indefatigable industry and widespread organization that explained what the San Francisco Chronicle called "the strange fondness of immigrants for the wet slopes of the Cascade Mountains and the solitary banks of the great Columbia." [14]

Oregon gained in the late 19th century by a California misfortune. The long legal wrangles over the Spanish and Mexican land grants created a feeling of title uncertainty which was anathema to the landowning instincts of the American pioneer. A letter written to the Oregonian in 1878 to promote settlement in eastern Clackamas and Marion Counties boasted that all original land titles in Oregon were perfect, with "* * * no Spanish grant or adverse legal claims." [15]

California was also the scene of vast land speculations involving high concentration of ownership, which aroused in Henry George his thoughts on the single tax. A California editor complained in 1869 that the existence of these holdings was retarding California growth while homeseekers went to Oregon and the Pacific Northwest.[16]

The early promotion "literature," while not hiding any Oregon lights under bushels, was dignified and sounded a note of caution to the overoptimistic. Around 1910, when the last available public land was in sight, the promotion "literature" threw all caution to the winds to play upon the fact that homestead land was almost gone. In an

[13] Benjamin MacLean Whitesmith, "Henry Villard and the Development of Oregon," University of Oregon Thesis Series No. 14 ([Eugene] [1942]), p. 12.

[14] Glenn Chesney Quiett, "They Built the West: An Epic of Rails and Cities" (New York, 1934), p. 370.

[15] The Oregonian, July 11, 1878.

[16] Ibid., Jan. 26, 1869.

early Villard pamphlet, "Pacific Northwest," a warning note was included:

> No one should think of emigrating without sufficient means of self-support for at least a short time after reaching his destination; for suitable employment immediately after arrival cannot always be relied upon, and there is nothing more discouraging to the newcomer than to become a subject of public or private charity. This caution applies particularly to heads of families, who would be cruelly derelict in their duty to expose those depending upon them to the risk of destitution upon arrival.[17]

Central Oregon, which had Bend for its center, was settled largely because of railroad penetration of that vastness. The Great Northern, which itself had no land to sell (as it was quick to state in its promotion leaflets), issued no warning about prospects in central Oregon. One pamphlet, "Oregon—320 Acres Free," played on the landowning instincts of the American with all stops out. The end of "free land" was clearly in sight when central Oregon was settled, and this fact was the focus of the land promotion argument. This brochure urged people to homestead in central Oregon before free land was gone.

> Prosperity is coming into Central Oregon by steam, down the tracks of the Oregon Trunk Railway. Why not go out and get your birthright, 320 free fertile acres, which can be left to your children forever and ever., The time is rapidly approaching when there will be no free land left. When this free land is gone, all other farmland will increase tremendously in value as to make it difficult to acquire.[18]

There were 10 million acres to be homesteaded in central Oregon, according to the pamphlet, but the settler must have the vision, it warned, to see the land as it could be, not as it was. To those without such vision, however, it was a land where, as the saying went, the jackrabbits packed lunches.

A Northern Pacific pamphlet described central Oregon as an "imperial domain" and "he who bravely takes time by the forelock, fares forth and establishes a home there, will not regret it." [19] Areas of eastern Oregon had been closed to settlement pending determination of forest reserve boundaries. When land was reopened to entry, the Great Northern would advertise it in promotion pamphlets giving general instructions for taking up land and cost of tickets from midwestern points.

Eastern Oregon was not the sole subject of this settlement promotion. To foster community development, more population was needed in the already settled regions of western Oregon. As one pamphlet pointed out, there were advantages, even though it cost money to buy improved property in western Oregon. Free Government land meant land away from railroads and schools.[20]

The temper of the times probably fostered the combination of fact and anticipated hope that passed for fact in these promotion bulletins. Western communities were under a compelling pressure to bring something near equilibrium between resources and a sufficiency of people to exploit them. Hopes mingled with hard fact. There was a characteristic overestimate of land values and a gross underestimate of the long, accumulative process of wealth production through rising land values.

---

[17] James B. Hedges, "Promotion of Immigration to the Pacific Northwest by Railroads," Mississippi Valley Historical Review, XV (1928), 201–202.
[18] Great Northern, "Oregon—320 Acres Free" (n.p., n.d.), p. 5.
[19] Northern Pacific, Central Oregon (n.p., n.d.), p. 19.
[20] Southern Pacific, "Oregon for the Settler" (Portland, n.d.), p. 6.

Land was being settled faster than the increasing population could profitably sustain it. In the later stages of western settlement much of the land was marginal. Disappointment was bound to follow its settlement. The urge to possess land, in the last stage of Oregon settlement, became irrational. The comparison between original and final homestead entries gives a statistical clue, but no statistic compares to seeing an abandoned homestead up a dry canyon in some remote corner of eastern Oregon.

HOMESTEADS IN EASTERN OREGON

The pathos of the American dream of a family freehold, fostered possibly by irresponsible advertising, being shattered on the arid plateaus of eastern Oregon has been caught by H. L. Davis, Oregon-born novelist, in his "Back to the Land—Oregon 1907" in the American Mercury.[21] Davis describes a homesteading season he witnesses as a young boy in one of the cow towns of eastern Oregon.

It is an unhappy event he describes. The homesteaders had been arriving in the cow town, a few wagons at a time, having driven 200 miles through the spring mud.

> And they were not much to look at. They were coming to take up farms, which the Government was willing to give away; and everybody in the country knew that there were no farms worth having as a gift * * *. Not knowing that, or that their 200 miles of mud wallowing were useless, the homesteaders were pitiable; and the sight of a pitiable man is embarrassing.

Davis worked for a drink-loving country editor who interviewed all homesteaders upon arrival.

> I had to set in type the stories about them which the editor banged off whenever a wagon struggled into town, and it griped my sense of honesty even to read such a set of lies, false surmises, and impossible predictions as he let loose about them * * *.

Davis allows a ranch foreman to explain the psychology of this latter day homesteading:

> It's one of the things we figger on about every 10 years. It ain't anything a man can help.
>
> They don't run on sense, like ordinary homesteadin'. They can't because there ain't any sense to them. A homestead rush runs on what old timers used to call afflatus. It's a kinda edge, you might say, and they have to keep goin' till they git it worked out * * *.
>
> Any of them tell you how the rush started? They seen an advertisement. You know what kind of people answer advertisement, don't you? * * *.
>
> As individuals they were simple enough to understand. A set of misfits, who had come homesteading because they could not be worse off, and they would try anything once. But, collectively, they had the weight and dignity of some great force of nature * * *.
>
> There was another anomaly. They had gone to so much work and misery to get in before the good claims were taken, and when they got there they took anything that happened to be close * * * *.
>
> Since then I have seen the same thing happen many times. If there is any reason for it in nature, I don't know what it is. Race-abberation, maybe; or a holdover from an instinct that did once have some sense to it. One guess is as good as another. The ranch foreman probably hit as close as any when he called it afflatus * * *.
>
> We used to hear them when they moved out, passing the cattle ranch in the night, arguing to make their wives stop crying, and explaining that there was still a new section of country a couple of hundred miles farther on, where a man stood a chance.

[21] H. L. Davis, "Back to the Land—Oregon, 1907," American Mercury, XVI (1929). The quotations are taken from pp. 315–318, 321–323.

The Oregonian news columns of 1895 tell of land boomers passing through Portland on their way from a land opening on the Siletz Reservation where they found nothing to please them. They were on their way to Alberta "* * * about which they seem to know as little as they did about the Siletz Reservation." [22]

Theoretically, settlers could not move onto land until the vacant public lands had been surveyed. In actuality, surveying never kept up with the insistent demands of settlement. There cannot be really sound titles until land has been surveyed as a basis for legal descriptions, therefore the rate of survey was a keen preoccupation of the Oregon settlers. Prior to survey, a man could hold a quarter-section by "squatter sovereignty," that is, by the preemption right. This was secure enough, but no American settler felt fully secure until his land had been patented by the United States. There seemed to be in Oregon in the latter decades of the 19th century an ever present fear that the lands of settlers might fall into the hands of unscrupulous land monopolists.

Oregon surveys seemed to lag most acutely in the 1870's to judge by the complaints voiced in the Oregonian in that decade. The annual surveying appropriation was between $25,000 and $30,000, which was far from adequate. Oregon topography caused an inequitable distribution of surveying. Contractors were willing enough to take work in the open country of eastern Oregon at the mileage rate in the appropriation acts but shunned the heavily timbered regions of western Oregon.[23] Easterners in Congress were unwilling to appropriate more although the rate for surveying heavy timber was increased to $16 per mile.[24]

IRRIGATION AND RECLAMATION

Irrigation was a new and intriguing feature of the later settlement of Oregon. Eastern Oregon, in common with the arid West, saw irrigation as its salvation. And within its limits, irrigation can accomplish veritable miracles. Early enthusiasts may have been led to expectations beyond accomplishments, but accomplishments were great in themselves.

Private limited attempts at irrigation in Oregon date back to 1869. A national attempt to foster private irrigation was the Desert Land Act of 1877 which permitted the purchase of 640 acres by an applicant if he could irrigate a portion of the section. A second national move to promote western irrigation was the Carey Act of 1894. This act authorized the granting of land to the arid States, to a maximum of 1 million acres per State, if the State would assume the obligation of its reclamation and sale to settlers. Oregon accepted the terms of the Carey Act in 1901 and immediately initiated 20 projects, although only two had been carried to completion by 1911. Oregon applied for the withdrawal from private entry of 791,615 acres for development under the Carey Act; only 276,403 were withdrawn by the Federal Government; and 73,442 were actually patented to the State of Oregon.[25] The disparity between the requested withdrawal and the land patented is a measure of the limited success

[22] The Oregonian, July 1, 1895.
[23] The Oregonian, Apr. 13, 1871.
[24] The Oregonian, Apr. 13, 1871.
[25] Report of the Director of the Bureau of Land Management, 1950, Statistical Appendix, p. 128.

in irrigation to be attained through private construction. Reclamation was taken in the West as a great panacea, and characteristically, the problems, engineering and economic, were underestimated.

Private companies did the construction work on these Carey Act projects. The State merely exercised certain supervisory powers. As their reports warned prospective settlers, the State of Oregon did not guarantee any company.[26] A desert land board, composed of the Governor, attorney general, and State engineer, was created in 1909. Originally, Carey Act projects had been under the supervision of the State land board, which had neither the experience nor the time to deal with engineering facets of irrigation projects.

The early projects, initiated before the desert land board was functioning, suffered from financial difficulties, irresponsible promotion, lack of sufficient water supply, inherent nonfeasibility, and an element of land speculation.[27] There were overestimates of water supply, underestimates of the amount of water needed to reclaim land, and an underestimation of the costs of reclamation.[28] The record of 73,000 irrigated acres is a mark of limited success in a field where private individual construction was basically not feasible on any grand scale.

In 1902 the Federal Government passed to the last great step in western reclamation, a Federal reclamation program. Reclamation had not been uniformly successful, at least on a large scale, through private means and the West turned to the Federal Government for aid in development. The Newlands Act has been amended several times, but in essence it calls for the United States to underwrite reclamation construction by assuming the costs which will be ultimately repaid without interest by settlers on irrigated land.

There have been sizable Bureau of Reclamation projects in Oregon. The Klamath project, partly in California, uses the upper Klamath Lake for storage and has reclaimed the lower Klamath and Tule Lakes for irrigated crops. Another Oregon project is the Owyhee in eastern Oregon, part of which is in Idaho. The land of these reclamation projects was withdrawn from public entry and then, as construction proceeded, the land was opened to settlement. The land is patented under the Homestead Act, but there are restrictions and special qualifications to meet Bureau of Reclamation standards, including certain preferences to war veterans.

POPULATION INCREASE

If there has been one common denominator in the American century in Oregon, it is that of an increasing population bringing into closer balance people and natural resources. In the beginning were the farmers of the Mississippi Valley, bent on receiving a 640-acre competence in the open valleys of western Oregon. Later, were the cattle and sheepmen of eastern Oregon, closely followed by the railroad sponsored homesteader. After 1890, were the timber cruisers for the midwestern lumbermen. Not many years behind the cruisers was that rough and picturesque breed, the lumberjack. And the latest increment might well be characterized by the industrial workers,

[26] [Oregon] Desert Land Board, 2d Biennial Report, 1913, p. 8.

[27] S. Doc. No. 1097. 62d Cong., 3d sess., p. 16.

[28] [Oregon] Desert Land Board, 3d Biennial Report, 1915, p. 3. A view strongly opposed to reclamation is Ray P. Teele, "The Economics of Land Reclamation in the United States" (New York, 1927).

recruited in the east and hurried west by Henry J. Kaiser to build Liberty ships on the shipways of Portland in World War II.

Oregon census returns

Year	Number	Increase	Percent
1850	12,093		
1860	52,645	39,171	295
1870	90,923	38,458	73
1880	174,768	83,845	92
1890	317,704	142,936	81
1900	413,536	95,832	30
1910	672,765	259,229	62
1920	783,389	110,624	16
1930	953,786	170,397	21
1940	1,089,684	135,898	14
1950	1,521,341	431,657	39
1960 [1]	1,757,691	236,350	15

[1] Preliminary estimate.

CHAPTER III

EXTINGUISHING THE INDIAN TITLE

The clash between civilized and barbaric peoples is tragic in the full Greek sense that antagonist and protagonist are bound by circumstances and forces which they may not circumvent. There are no felicitous resolutions. It is heightened when the barbaric peoples foredoomed to defeat possess the determination, courage, and skill to fight to a bitter end. The 300-year struggle on the North American Continent between expanding Europeans and the aborigines is a prime instance of the heightened tragedy. To approach this long struggle without its tragic essense well in mind is to bog down in sentimentality over the plight of the vanquished or fruitless deprecation of the conquerors. There is no justice in such situations. The sense of justice must reconcile itself to ameliorations.

In its relations with the Indian tribes within or near its jurisdictions, the Government of the United States was acutely conscious of its reponsibility for the promotion of equitable dealing. Before the Federal Government would convey any of its lands to private individuals, it was firm in its stand that (1) the lands be surveyed by Government surveyors; (2) titles granted by other sovereign powers be confirmed; (3) the Indian title, however vague, be extinguished. In short, the Federal Government was insistent that it hold an impeccable title before conveyance. Needless to say, these requirements, whose fulfilling was often time consuming, could not be met with the rapidity demanded by American expansion.

In acquiring title to Indian land the Government acted until 1872 on the legal fiction that each tribe was a sovereign nation. Consequently, when joint occupation of the vast and varied Oregon country ended in 1846 with the United States in full possession of the region between the 42d and 49th parallels, the Rocky Mountains and the Pacific Ocean, the task of extinguishing of the Indian title, in keeping with its longstanding policy, was presented to the Federal Government.

Negotiations for Indian cessions were never easy. In Oregon an added complication was the presence of settlers on the scene before the Central Government. With the tide of settlement running previous to cession parleys, peaceful relations snapped. The Yakima and Rogue River Wars grew directly from the mishandling of extinguishment negotiations.

DELAYED EXTINGUISHMENT

Although the early settlers in Oregon and their provisional government could not negotiate with the Indians for their lands, they promised the Willamette Valley tribes that they would be compensated when the Federal Government extended its sovereignty to Oregon, as negotiations for land cessions were strictly a function of the Central

Government.[1] Although it was Government policy to extinguish Indian title, in Oregon's case however, it was the Willamette Valley settlers who evinced the greatest desire that the title be properly purchased. The procrastination of the Federal Government was, therefore, a matter of grave concern to Oregonians, for it promoted Indian unrest. One early petition complained of neglect and expressed fear of a general Indian war if the promises to the tribes were not acted upon.

> We do not complain—

wrote the petitioners—

> of oppression but of *neglect*. Even the tyrant has his moments of relaxation and kindness, but neglect never wears a smile.[2]

As early as 1848 the call for action was strongly voiced. One of the numerous editors of the Oregon Spectator, the territory's first newspaper, lambasted the Central Government for its failure to seek extinguishment of the Indian title. The Waiilatpu massacre and resulting Cayuse War—

> * * * were mainly and unmistakably attributable to the unjustifiable neglect of the Government of the United States * * *. Every page of the history of every State in the Union warned Congress of the necessity of early extinguishing the Indian title to lands upon which settlements had been made by whites, and protecting those settlements by the strong arm of military power.[3]

The Willamette Valley tribes were anxious to sell their rights to the United States. They sensed the futility of resistance and sought only the compensation which had been promised. Their concern was that they might be driven into extinction before its payment. Joseph Lane, first territorial Governor and Superintendent of Indian Affairs, has described how Indians besieged him upon his arrival:

> * * * as soon as it was known among the numerous tribes * * * bordering the settlements that the Governor had arrived, they flocked in * * * chiefs, headmen, warriors * * * entire bands—expecting presents; making known what the whites had promised * * * that when the laws of the United States were extended over Oregon the Governor would bring them blankets, shirts * * *. Although disappointed at not receiving presents they evinced a feeling of friendship toward us, and generally expressed a desire to sell their possessory rights to any portion of their country that our Government should wish to purchase.[4]

The first subject of Lane's first speech to the Territorial legislature was the necessity of extinguishing the Indian claims. The initial authorization to deal with the tribes was engineered in 1850 by Oregon Territory's first Congressional Delegate, Samuel Thurston, who secured passage of an act in 1850, to extinguish the Indian title west of the Cascade Mountains.[5] It provided for the appointment of three commissioners to negotiate, separated the office of Superin-

[1] The Confederation government was expressly the only agency authorized to treat with Indian tribes for land cessions. "* * * and they [the Confederation Congress] do hereby prohibit and forbid all persons from making settlements on lands inhabited or claimed by Indians, * * *, and from purchasing or receiving any gift or cession of such lands or claims without express authority and direction of the United States in Congress assembled." Journals of the Continental Congress, Library of Congress edition, XXV, p. 602.

The United States clearly reserved for itself the function of obtaining Indian cessions. See Act "to regulate Trade and Intercourse with the Indian Tribes," Stat. L., I, 330.

The act creating Oregon Territory expressly stated that the act was not to be construed as impairing the rights of person or property pertaining to Indians "* * * so long as such rights shall remain unextinguished by treaty between the United States and such Indians." Ibid., IX, p. 323.

[2] Oregon Spectator, Oct. 14, 1847.

[3] Ibid., Dec. 28, 1848.

[4] "Senate Executive Documents," 31st Cong., 2d sess., No. 1, p. 156.

[5] Stat. L., IX, 437. Oregon was well represented in Samuel Thurston. In connection with this bill, one observer said of him, "* * * I question whether as tactician or debater combined, he has a superior in Congress, except the Speaker * * *," Oregon Spectator, Aug. 22, 1850.

tendent of Indian Affairs from the governorship of Oregon Territory, and contemplated the removal of western Oregon Indians to a permanent haven east of the Cascades. The removal was never made, principally because the marked physical differences between eastern and western Oregon did not make this scheme at all feasible.

Three Commissioners were appointed.[6] Anson Dart was named first Superintendent of Indian Affairs. He was the driving force in the ensuing parleys. Though the activities of Dart and his Commissioners were extensive, they were abortive. Congress did not ratify his 13 treaties with the coast and Willamette Valley tribes. The tribes treated with were small;[7] they could not be prevailed upon to move east of the mountains, so Dart created reserves within the ceded areas, an action which did not meet with the approval of settlers. And one treaty, possibly the most important for it included the populous sector of the Willamette Valley, was framed by Dart, without the Commissioners present. The 13 unratified treaties involved 6 million acres which would have been procured at something near 2 cents per acre.[8]

JOEL PALMER'S NEGOTIATIONS

With appointment of Joel Palmer as Superintendent of Indian Affairs, Oregon Territory, the task of obtaining the Indian cessions was finally successfully begun. The mid-years of the 1850's were the years of the major activity in this endeavor. In rapid succession between 1853 and 1855 treaties were completed with the Rogue Rivers, Shastas, Umpquas, Calapooias, the Confederated Bands of the Willamette Valley, the Walla Walla, the Umatillas, Cayuse, Nez Percés, and the Confederated Tribes of Middle Oregon and the Molalas.[9]

The treaties with the Walla Walla, Umatilla, Cayuse and Nez Percé nations were negotiated jointly with Isaac Stevens, Governor and Superintendent of Indian Affairs for Washington Territory (created 1853). To obtain these cessions a big council was held at Walla Walla, Washington Territory, in June 1855. These fierce, proud tribes signed the cessions with reluctance. The Walla Walla treaties were not ratified by the Senate until 1859, and this delay was the overt cause of a period of general war and unrest in the Northwest during 1855–1858. Shortly after the Walla Walla council, Palmer arranged treaties with the Oregon coastal tribes which were never ratified although administration of affairs was carried out as though they had been.[10]

In the 1860's a further cession from the Nez Percé, a settlement with the Klamaths, Modocs, and two bands of the Snakes completed the extinguishment of the Indian title in Oregon. There remained

[6] Commissioners were J. P. Gaines, Alonzo H. Skinner and Beverly Allen. "Senate Executive Documents," 31st Cong., 2d sess., No. 1, pp. 145–151.

[7] One of the Chinook bands with which Dart made a treaty consisted of two adult males. Coan, loc. cit., p. 59.

[8] Oregon Spectator, Nov. 11, 1851. For detailed accounts of Dart's negotiations see Coan, loc. cit., pp. 46–89.

[9] See appendix for dates and treaty provisions.

[10] Bureau of Ethnology, Eighteenth Annual Report, II, 812, 814, 839, 879; pl. No. 51, tracts 397, 578, 579, 479. In 1951 several bands of coast tribes won a suit against the Federal Government for damages arising from the lack of compensation for lands covered by these unratified treaties. These tribes have been awarded, by the Supreme Court on Apr. 9, 1951, $3,527,096 as the value of 2,772,580 acres at $1.20 per acre. The claim plus interest amounted to $16,515,574 by January 1950, but the Supreme Court disallowed the interest. *Alsea Band of Tillamooks et al.* v. *U.S.*, 103 Court of Claims 494; 115 Court of Claims 463; 71 S. Ct. 552. Also The Oregonian, Oct. 23, 1947; Oct. 25, 1947.

a good deal of adjusting and modifying of reservation boundaries, but that is a story unto itself.

The record of these cessions is one of war, intrigue, promises broken or delayed in fulfilment. The purchase of Indian title can in no way be envisioned as a free sale where the seller did not have to sell or the buyer did not have to buy. The tribes east of the Cascades quite definitely did not want to sell; only with reluctance did they make their cessions. When payments were not forthcoming, they turned to war of extermination to resist encroachment of American settlers.

Keeping settlement back from areas where the Indian nations had not relinquished their claims had been a problem to the Central Government since it had taken over the Crown Lands of Britain. In the Oregon Country the problem was acute, because, as has been mentioned, settlement preceded the sovereignity of the United States. In fact, many if not all, the Willamette Valley settlers came out to that fertile land to win it for the United States; and these people expected generous reward in land. They were, therefore, anxious to see the Indian title extinguished. The valley settlers had from the beginning promised that the Indian title would be purchased by the United States and the Willamette Valley tribes were quite willing to sell.

In southern and eastern Oregon no such happy solution was manifest. The tribes did not relish a forced sale. Being fierce and proud they were not loath to risk war. And in their case the whites did not show any consideration toward Indian rights of occupancy. In one instance the Cayuse lands were declared forfeit by the superintendent of Indian affairs for the Oregon provisional government and subject to white settlement.[11] The treaties of June 1855 were jeopardized by an announcement inferring that the cessions were open to settlement before the Senate ratified the treaties and payments were made.[12] A gold strike in the Colville area of eastern Washington and mining activity in the Rogue River country of Oregon were unpropitious irritants.

UNRATIFIED TREATIES AND THE YAKIMA WAR

Affairs called for direct and immediate attention. It was not forthcoming. Failure to act must lie with the Central Government. In the first instance it was slow to authorize the preliminaries to extinguishing the title. Secondly, it left, for unaccountable reasons, the Walla Walla treaties unratified for 4 years.[13] In the interim a fierce war was waged in the Northwest. While the Central Government took its time the tribes were apprehensive over the movement toward their lands. They had been reluctant to negotiate in the first place. They needed, therefore, no added incentive to their one recourse—war of extermination.

Three years of border war was consequently the price paid for a settlement based exactly upon the treaties of 1855 which, following

[11] The proclamation of July 6, 1848, read in part: "In consideration of the barbarities and insufferable conduct of the Cayuse indians [sic] as portrayed in the massacre of American families at Waiilatpu, and the subsequent cause of the hostilities against Americans generally, and with a view to inflict upon them a just and proper punishment, as well as to secure and protect our fellow citizens immigrating from the United States to this territory against a course of reckless aggression so long and so uniformly practiced upon them by the said Cayuse indians [sic] * * * I, H. A. G. Lee, Superintendent Indian Affairs [Oregon Provisional Government] hereby declare the territory of said Cayuse indians [sic] forfeited by them, and justly subject to be held by American residents in Oregon * * *." Oregon Spectator, July 13, 1848.

[12] Oregon Weekly Times, June 23, 1855, quoted in Carey, "History of Oregon," p. 588.

[13] Congressional documents are singularly devoid of any references to these Walla Walla treaties. They were passed at a Senate executive session Mar. 8, 1859.

the war, were ratified in 1859. A major portion of blame must be carried by Congress.[14] It did not seem to appreciate the problem created by the imminence of white settlement. It had been repeatedly warned that a willy-nilly handling of title extinguishment would lead to a general Indian war.

CONGRESSIONAL RESPONSIBILITY

There seems to be only one apparent reason for this inattention—Congress was not fully accustomed to dealing with all the diverse problems created by the acquisition of lands from Britain and Mexico. The years 1850–60 were turbulent, with much pressing upon congressional minds. After all, the Indian title to a far-off region like Oregon was bound to yield attention to such provocative issues as slavery and States rights.

This lack of decisive action and the frequent change of those in authority did not go unnoticed by wily Indian chiefs. One chief, who had remained at peace during the Rogue War and wished to be well rewarded, twitted one official observer about the tenure of office in a republic.

> One superintendent tells us another thing, and another big chief removes him. Who are we to believe? Who is your great chief and who is to tell us the truth. We don't understand the way you act. With us we are born chief; once a chief we are a chief for life. But you are only common man and we never know how long you will hold your authority, or how soon the great chief may degrade you, or how soon he may be turned out himself. We want to know the true head that we may state our condition to him.[15]

As the story of Indian cessions in Oregon unfolded, it followed a pattern cut in colonial times: divergence between Government policy and settler policy. The Government hoped and attempted to hold back the currents of settlement from Indian country. Always the dynamics of land hunger won out and the Government was forced to give way before its citizens and execute new arrangements with the tribes. Settlers themselves probably thought this was an overscrupulous consideration for Indian rights. Consciously or unconsciously the settlers operated on what was for them a "higher law," that unsettled, untilled land was God-given for those who would work it.

In eastern Washington and Oregon (the area ceded by the Walla Walla treaties), the Army made a determined effort to keep out settlers until the treaties were ratified. In 1856 Maj. Gen. John Wool, commanding general, Department of the Pacific, issued instructions to his officers in Oregon and Washington Territories that—

> no emigrants or other whites * * * will be permitted to settle or remain in the Indian country, on land not ceded by treaty confirmed by the Senate and signed by the President of the United States.[16]

In the same instructions he directed that a detachment of volunteers known to be headed toward Walla Walla were to be ordered out of Indian country and if they did not comply they were to be disarmed and sent out.

[14] For congressional inattention to legislation, see Allan Nevins, "Ordeal of the Union" (New York, 1947), I, 163.
[15] "House Executive Documents," 35th Cong., 1st sess., No. 39, p. 27.
[16] "House Executive Documents," 34th Cong., 3d sess., No. 1, pt. 2, p. 169.

ENCROACHMENT UPON INDIAN LAND

General Wool's successor, N. S. Clarke, issued a similar order prohibiting settlement east of the Salmon River in Washington and the Deschutes in Oregon.[17] Needless to say, the reaction from settlers was soon forthcoming. The Washington territorial legislature sent a memorial to Congress. In language unmistakably reflecting frontier reaction to interference with its expansive nature, it declared:

> Whereas certain officers of the United States Army have unlawfully assumed to issue orders prohibiting citizens of this Territory from settling certain portions thereof, and * * * have driven citizen settlers from their claims and homes acquired under the laws of the United States—to their great injury * * *.
>
> Therefore, be it resolved * * * in our opinion, the said orders are without the authority of law and that the acts done under such orders are a highhanded outrage upon the rights and liberties of the American people.
>
> * * * proclaimed by tyrants not having the feeling in common with us, nor interests identified with ours.[18]

The treaties ceding the region had not at that time been ratified, and therefore, the land laws of the United States were hardly applicable except that Congress itself, in 1858, a year before the cession treaties were ratified, extended the land laws of the United States to the region east of the Cascades,[19] which meant in effect that the lands were open for settlement. Earlier in the decade, the passage of a Donation Land Act confused the Indian title extinguishment picture by providing a generous land grant which led to encroachment upon lands to which Indian rights had not been acquired.

A constant source of embarrassment and shame to Indian agents and less excitable citizens was the action, particularly in southern Oregon, of unofficial enforcers of the American conquest. Among the southern Oregon mining element were "miscreants" whose activities smacked of more savagery than that practiced by the Indians. In one case, one of these avenging bands fell upon a friendly band of treaty Indians encamped upon their own reserve and killed without respect to age or sex.[20] This and like activities brought from the adjutant general of Oregon Territory the judgment that—

> a partisan warfare against any band of Indians within our borders or on our frontiers is pregnant only with mischief, and will be viewed with distrust and disapprobation by every citizen who values the peace and good order of the settlements.[21]

This indiscriminate killing stirred hatred and nullified the peacemaking activities of Indian agents. Joel Palmer, who concluded the bulk of the Oregon cession treaties, made constant reference to the misdeeds of whites. Palmer laid the blame for the Rogue War directly upon "miscreants."

To protect friendly Indians from further barbarous attacks, Palmer advocated and executed their removal to reservations in western Oregon. The Grande Ronde Reservations in the foothills west of the Willamette Valley and the Coast (later the Siletz) Reservation were

---

17 Ibid., 35th Cong., 1st sess., No. 112, p. 3; Carey, "History of Oregon," p. 620.
18 "House Executive Documents," 35th Cong., 2d sess., No. 2, pt. 2, pp. 341–342.
19 Stat. L., XI, 293.
20 "House Executive Documents," 34th Cong., 1st sess., No. 93, pp. 75–76.
21 "Senate Executive Documents," 34th Cong., 1st sess., No. 26, pp. 10–11.

established as permanent havens for the tribesmen.[22] In the early months of the Rogue War, Palmer's chief concern was for the protection of the Indians under his charge.

Palmer's policy of removing tribesmen from contact with civilization had its opponents. Willamette Valley settlers did not react favorably to establishing Indians near the valley. In fact, the claims of some settlers had to be purchased in the site selected as the Grand Ronde Reservation. The Oregon territorial legislature in a memorial to Congress asked for his dismissal not only because of his Indian policy but because of an asserted political perfidy in representing himself as a "sound national democrat" who had turned to the Know-Nothings.

Palmer also reconnoitered eastern Oregon for reservation sites for western Oregon Indians, presumably beyond the limits of settlements. He selected the Klamath country as an ideal place for their removal. His plan did not materialize, although in 1870 the largest reservation in the State was created there by the cession treaty with the Klamaths.

If the conquest of a less advanced race by a more advanced is essentially tragic, the act played in Oregon contained the elements of the larger tragedy. As the resolution was worked out in Oregon, it might be said to be as happy a one as any tragic solution is allowed to be. The rich and varied land which Americans were bound to have (by their destiny, if you will) was acquired for the expansion of western civilization. The Indians were provided havens and the blows against their lives and culture were so modified that their race was not ground into abysmal extinction.

KLAMATH TERMINATION

In 1953 the Congress announced its intention to proceed to the termination of the Government trust relation with "tribes, groups, and individual Indians as rapidly as the circumstances of each * * * will permit * * *."[23] Oregon's Klamaths were among the first to benefit from the Government's new direction in its long history of dealing with Indians. The Klamath Termination Act of 1954 (68 Stat. 718) was passed to solve one set of problems—the trust relationships between the Government and tribes and members of tribes but in so doing brought on another set. The new problems, apparently solved by a later act, gathered around the disposition of the ponderosa timber holdings of the Klamaths. The 800,000 acres of the Klamath Forest encompass probably the best remaining stand of ponderosa and sugar pine in the Nation.[24]

When the original Klamath Termination Act was under discussion in the Committee on Interior and Insular Affairs in both the House and Senate it was generally assumed that few members of the tribe would avail themselves of the right conferred by the act to elect to withdraw from the tribe and have their interest in the tribal property converted to cash. Instead over three-quarters of the 2,133 members elected to withdraw.[25] The principal asset to be converted was the timber. To have followed the procedure of the basic act, 3.5 billion

[22] The removal was made under troop protection. It is somewhat analogous to the movement of the Japanese from the Pacific coast in 1942.

[23] S. Rept. 1631, 83d Cong., 1st sess., p. 3.

[24] Ibid., p. 8.

[25] S. Rept. 1518, 85th Cong., 2d sess., p. 6.

board feet of timber and 1,400,000 cords of pulpwood from the tribal patrimony would have had to have been placed on sale within 2 years. In other words the prospect was placed before the timber industry in the Klamath Basin of absorbing in 2 years a quantity of timber equivalent to 60 percent of the annual timber cut for the United States. The sale of national forest timber would be disrupted, the Senate Committee on Interior and Insular Affairs was told by the Forest Service; local mills dependent upon a continuing availability of Klamath Indian timber might be denied access, the Klamaths themselves would suffer. In general an unhealthy situation all the way around was predicted.

The problem was set squarely before Congress in 1957. Fortunately for all the interests involved, Richard L. Neuberger, junior Senator from Oregon, took over in 1957 as chairman of the Indian Affairs Subcommittee of the Senate Committee on Interior and Insular Affairs, the group which would have to deal most directly with issue. In this position he guided through the 85th Congress a solution to the impasse.

The amending act (72 Stat. 816) provided for the orderly disposition of this important asset by the following procedure: Placing the timber for sale to private bidders who would agree to manage the timber on a sustained yield basis and otherwise engage in conservation practices, such bidders to bid at least the realization value of the timber, which was defined as the fair market value had it been placed for competitive sale during the 7 years ending August 1961 without such limitations as the sustained yield requirement. In the event that such bidding did not secure successful bidders the law provided for the United States to purchase the timberland at the realization value, to the extent of $90 million and to organize the Klamath timberlands as a new national forest. The act further provided for the purchase by the Government of the 15,900 acres of the Klamath Marsh to be administered by the Secretary of the Interior as a wildlife refuge.

At the 1960 bidding the offers were below the minimum required by law. This was generally anticipated because the law required the payment of the going value of timber while it required at the same time that private bidders enter into agreements for sustained yield management. The private companies were not willing, as their bids showed, to pay the immediate value of timber for which there would be a long term of sustained yield cutting. It appears at this writing that the Government will take over the Klamath forest for a payment not in excess of $90 million and such timberlands will be organized as a new national forest under the acquired Forest Lands Act of 1911.

The payment to each individual member of the tribe electing to withdraw from the tribe and take his share in cash is expected to work out to be in the neighborhood of $50,000 per member, including children. Upon the completion of the conversion, the assets will be distributed and trust and other special relationships between the Klamaths and the Government will cease. Each will be on his own, fully equal before the law with a legacy bordering on $50,000.

At this writing it lacks but 4 years of a century since the Klamaths forsook their title to vast reaches of the high plateau and timbered ridges of eastern Oregon for the 1 million acres of the Klamath Reservation. In this century the 1 million acres of the reservation have passed through two distinct stages and in the process of a third and final stage. Before the treaty of 1864 the Klamaths exercised as a tribe right to use of a great somewhat undefined expanse of eastern Oregon. By the treaty of 1864 the Klamaths relinquished their title for an assured reservation of 1 million acres extending 45 miles east and 50 miles north of the marshy shores of the upper Klamath Lake.

A second stage came in wake of the General Allotment Act of 1887 under the terms of which 107,059 acres were allotted to individual members in fee simple title while another 137,028 acres were allotted but held in trust for individuals. The tribe itself retained ownership of 863,158 acres, 95 percent of which was the ponderosa pine forest. The forest has been placed for sale to the public under the terms of the Termination Act but all the indications are that the public, meaning the timber companies, are not going to exercise their rights and the United States will in the process acquire a new national forest.[26]

[26] The reports of the House and the Senate furnish an excellent summary of this situation. For the original act the reports are: S. Rept. 1631, 83d Cong., 2d sess., and H. Rept. 2483, 83d Cong., 2d sess. For the Neuberger amending act the reports are: S. Rept. 1518, 85th Cong., 2d sess.; H. Rept. 2278, 85thCong., 2d sess.; and H. Rept. 2544, 85th Cong., 2d sess.

CHAPTER IV

THE DONATION LAND ACT

THE LINN BILLS

The Donation Land Act, like so many of the land acts, had a long genesis. Land as a reward for settlement in Oregon was first brought into congressional halls in 1824 by John Floyd, a Virginia physician and friend of Thomas Hart Benton.[1] His bill created a territorial government, provided for the military occupation of Oregon, and offered a grant of land to induce settlement.[2] It passed the House, but no action was taken in the Senate. It brought no immediate result, but the pressure for acquisition of Oregon and for a land donation had been effectively initiated.

Successor to Floyd as protagonist for acquisition of Oregon was Lewis Linn, a Senator from Missouri from 1833 to 1843. Linn, whose background was similar to Floyd's (both were physicians with frontier experience) sponsored a series of bills to provide for the American advance into the Oregon country. In ardent support was his famous colleague, Thomas Hart Benton. Although Linn had "none of the arrogance and pomposity of his colleague, Benton; they were a strangely mated but effective pair." [3] One of Linn's bills passed the Senate in 1843.[4] While Linn's bills did not become law while he lived or while the joint occupation of the Oregon country was in effect, they were cited by proponents of an Oregon land donation act as a promise which had promoted the Oregon migrations. The bills and resolutions varied; they all included a land grant. Beginning in 1840, proposals included a 1,000-acre grant, a 640-acre grant, a 640-acre grant with an additional 160 acres for each child in a family.[5]

Emigration, however, did not wait on final passage. In Benton's mind the Senate-approved bill of 1843 was sufficient encouragement to "the enterprising people of the West." Oregon settlement demonstrated to Benton, writing in 1854, "how little the wisdom of government has to do with the great events which fix the fate of countries." [6]

As well they might be, two adjoining counties in the Willamette Valley were named for Benton and Linn as testimony to their legislative efforts.

Seven eventful years pressed themselves on American consciousness from Linn's last Oregon bill to the Donation Land Act of 1850. Great Britain ceded the Oregon country south of the 49th parallel, Mexico withdrew from the Southwest after the Mexican War and Oregon had been organized as a territory. Its first territorial delegate, Samuel Royal Thurston, was no Benton or Linn; but he was an indefatigable promoter of a Donation Land Act for his Oregon constituents. In

1 The Dictionary of American Biography (New York, 1931), VI, 481.
2 The Annals of the Congress of the United States, 18th Cong., 1st sess., p. 1084.
3 The Dictionary of American Biography, XI, 282.
4 The Congressional Globe, 27th Cong., 3d sess., p. 240.
5 "House Reports," 31st Cong., 1st sess., No. 271, pp. 2–3.
6 Thomas H. Benton, "Thirty Years' View" (New York, 1854), II, 477–478.

the East he interviewed editors, Congressmen, and executive officers, always urging a land grant.[7]

Thurston's baggage had been lost in crossing the Isthmus of Panama and in it were the memorials from the Oregon legislature. In lieu of these he offered two sets of resolutions in the House. One set, offered January 24, 1850, and directed against the Hudson's Bay Co. and the rights held by it under the treaty of 1846, was read for information only.[8] A second set was offered February 22, 1850. Their import was unmistakable. They directed the Committee on Territories: to inquire into the proportion of American citizens, foreigners, and those who had declared their intention to become citizens in the Oregon populace; to determine what first led to settlement; to ascertain the length of time a provisional government had been functioning at local expense; to report upon the hardships and inconveniences attendant to settlement in Oregon not peculiar to settlement east of the Rocky Mountains; and lastly, to inquire into "the propriety any justness of donating land to all American settlers now in said territord.[9] In other words the committee was directed to establish a record upon which the Donation Act could stand.

PASSAGE OF THE DONATION ACT

Congress found sufficient propriety and justness in a land donation, for on September 24, 1850, it passed—

An act to create the office of surveyor-general of the public lands in Oregon, and to provide for the survey, and to make donations to the settlers of the said public lands.[10]

The principal provision granted 320 acres to any white settler (including halfbreed Indians) who was a citizen of the United States (or declared his intention by December 1, 1851) residing in Oregon at the date of passage or arriving there by December 1, 1850, provided the individual would reside on and cultivate the tract for 4 years. A married man received 640 acres, one-half to be in his wife's own right.[11]

A grant one-half as large was made for those arriving in Oregon territory between December 1, 1850, and December 1, 1853; that is, 160 acres to a single man and 320 acres to a man and wife.

The Donation Act also granted two townships, amounting to 46,080 acres, west of the Cascades, one north and one south of the Columbia River, as support for a university. There were two amendatory acts. An act of February 14, 1853, extended the provisions of the main act to December 1, 1855. It further provided that an occupant could purchase the claim for $1.25 per acre after a 2-year residence upon it. After April 1, 1855, all public land west of the Cascades except donation claims, mineral lands and public reserves were subject to public sale.

An act of July 17, 1854, reduced occupancy to 1 year with a payment of $1.25 per acre. The sale of land prior to patent was recognized if the vendor had lived on it 4 years. In this act the preemption privilege was extended to Oregon and to Washington Territory.

---

[7] Samuel Royal Thurston, "Diary of Samuel Royal Thurston," O.H.Q., XV (1914), 153–205.
[8] The Congressional Globe, 31st Cong., 1st sess., p. 220.
[9] Ibid., p. 413.
[10] Stat. L., IX, 496.
[11] Stat. L., IX, 497.

CONGRESSIONAL DEBATE

It was formulated for a far-off western territory, but the Oregon Donation Act was a critical departure in public land policy. As such, it did not pass without opposition. Considerations of diplomacy had been arguments against the Linn bills. The joint occupation precluded in some minds, notably John C. Calhoun's,[12] the granting of land. He and others depended upon American expansion and frontier fecundity to win Oregon. The diplomatic objection was, of course, erased when Great Britain withdrew north of the 49th parallel.

An outright gift of public land was unprecedented and was attacked upon that ground. David L. Yulee, Senator from Florida, in the debate on the 1850 bill, spoke against it as being without precedent and as being a stimulus not given to any other territory. He attempted to strike out the clause granting land to those who emigrated to Oregon after 1850.[13]

There were other objections. It was foretold that it would complicate Indian title extinguishment, which it did.[14] The donation claims were authorized before adequate steps to extinguish Indian title had been made.

Isaac P. Walker, who represented Wisconsin in the Senate, spoke out against the largesse of a 640-acre grant. He told the Senate that later comers would not thank the Senate for granting entire sections to the first comers.[15] One attempt to make the donation claims immune from court judgment during the existence of Oregon Territory was voted down.[16]

THE DONATION ACT AND THE HUDSON'S BAY CO.

The Donation Act was used by an influential element in Oregon to strike at the Hudson's Bay Co. and its personification in the Oregon Country, Dr. John McLoughlin. The company and its subsidiary, The Puget Sound Agricultural Co., were the greatest land claimants in Oregon. Their land rights, as well as those of British citizens in general, were specifically protected in the 1846 treaty. Oregon settlers resented these holdings and threatened their retention.

The first territorial delegate, Samuel Royal Thurston, was spokesman for the anti-Hudson's Bay faction. He pushed his attack against the company and McLoughlin in an early congressional appearance. On January 24, 1850, he attempted to introduce resolutions in lieu of the memorials of the Oregon Legislature lost en route to Washington.[17] In this he exceeded his instructions.[18]

When the Donation Act was passed it struck decisively at McLoughlin, retired executive of the Hudson's Bay Co., who had developed a claim at the falls of the Willamette (Oregon City) and sold town lots from his claim. Thurston inserted a clause in the act which precluded a person from holding a claim under the Donation Act and simultaneously holding it under the cession treaty of 1846. McLoughlin was not an American citizen, although he had filed declaration; he was no longer a British citizen. This threw a

[12] The Congressional Gobe, 27th Cong., 3d sess., p. 134.
[13] The Congressional Globe, 31st Cong., 1st sess., p. 1841.
[14] The Congressional Globe, 31st Cong., 1st sess., p. 1077.
[15] The Congressional Globe, 31st Cong., 1st sess., p. 1843.
[16] Ibid.
[17] The Congressional Globe, 31st Cong., 1st sess., p. 220.
[18] Hubert Howe Bancroft, "Works" (San Francisco, 1886–88), XXX, 116.

cloud on his title from which it did not emerge in his lifetime.[19] The legal fight which ensued is not germane, but the attack upon McLoughlin's holdings was totally unwarranted. He had not opposed American migration to Oregon. He sold provisions on credit to Americans against company policy and left its service in 1846 under criticism.[20]

IMPORTANCE OF THE ACT

Fortunately the attack on McLoughlin was a minor part of the Donation Act. Its major achievement was a reward and inducement for emigration to Oregon where "nature was lavish and the Government munificent." Whether Americans would have made such a migration without the promise of a generous land grant is academic. The land was offered and the people came and 7,432 early settlers claimed 2,614,082 Oregon acres for their reward.[21]

The acreage figure itself does not adequately convey the impact upon Oregon. These donation claims were laid out in the valleys of western Oregon, the first settled and, to this day, the most populous. The donation claims embraced the Rogue, Umpqua, and Willamette Valleys. They included nearly all the open valley land of western Oregon.[22] Such largesse was a mixed blessing in the opinion of Hubert Howe Bancroft, the historian of the Pacific slope.[23] It encouraged slothfulness, rapacity, and stirred hopes for an unearned increment; surveying extortions drained $25,000 from the pockets of settlers. The size of the claims fostered scattered settlement making "population sparse and schooling dear." In the view of such a competent observer as Harvey W. Scott, 40 years the editor of the Oregonian, the claims were generous beyond the capacity to digest.

> If ever land greed could be excused (and whether excused or not it is one of the characteristics of our race), it was when it was given the chance to feed upon the smiling areas of the Willamette Valley * * * and feed it did, though the farming interests of the valley have as yet [1899] scarcely recovered from the * * * banquet at which each guest was encouraged to swallow more than he could digest.[24]

Fifty years after the Donation Act, T. W. Davenport, Oregon pioneer, one time State land agent and father of Homer Davenport, the famous cartoonist, closely examined 100 square miles on the east side of the Willamette Valley in Marion County.[25] He found that 66 percent of the donation claims had passed from the original claimants or their descendants, 15 percent were mortgaged for all they were worth, not more than 15 percent had kept the family holdings and made improvements, and 5 percent had increased their holdings. Significantly, Davenport discovered that those on 320-acre grants had held their own better than those on the larger ones. Davenport accounted for this state of affairs by overextension of credit, a careless attitude by descendants, the attraction of professional life away from the "old homestead" and the lure of cattle ranching in eastern Oregon.

The Donation Act was very successful in that it came very near to meeting the classic homestead ideal—award of the best farmland to the actual settlers. The first donation claim was filed February 18,

[19] Bancroft, "Works," XXX, 125–127.
[20] The Dictionary of American Biography, XII, 134–135.
[21] "Senate Documents," 58th Cong., 3d sess., No. 189, p. 140.
[22] Harvey W. Scott, "History of the Oregon Country" (Cambridge [Mass.], 1924), II, 90.
[23] Bancroft, "Works," XXX, 294.
[24] Scott, "History of the Oregon Country," I, 260.
[25] T. W. Davenport, loc. cit., pp. 50–51.

1852, by Joseph M. Blackberry for a tract 16 miles east of Salem in the Waldo Hills.[26] The donation claims precluded large-scale speculation in the Willamette Valley such as took place in the Mississippi Valley.[27] With each claimant holding 640 acres he was his own speculator, which, however, did not meet the approval of the Oregonian. An editorial, in 1862, expressed the fear that the donation claims would retard Willamette Valley settlement because new settlers would seek homesteads in remoter regions rather than pay a high price for donation claims in the valley.[28] The editor urged donation claim owners to place a reasonable price, in the interest of community development, upon their holdings.

Twenty years later, Scott still had cause to complain that certain donation claimholders refused to sell their land although they lived in indolence and without common conveniences.[29]

It is almost gratuitous to report that the double portion to man and wife promoted early marriage on the Oregon frontier. Early marriage was a frontier characteristic and it certainly received no damper with the Donation Act. One author has recorded a marriage of a girl of 12, although, he explains, the child bride spent a few more years at home.[30]

The double portion which went to the married stirred the levity of the editor of the Oregon Spectator. Writing about a walk through the countryside in 1851, he noted that some of the claims were not well kept:

> * * * and the time of the bachelors being greatly occupied in trying to secure the whole *grant*, is sufficient excuse in many instances for the unimproved condition. There is the greatest buzzing among the bachelor portion of the lords of the soil, ever witnessed in any country.[31]

Later in the year the deadline for getting another 320 acres via marriage was nearing, and the editor warned the young men and bachelors that:

> * * * the first day of December 1851 is near at hand. Your days of grace soon expire, and the 320 acres lost beyond redemption, unless you are up and stirring. The ladies, it seems to us, should wear their most winning smiles, and encourage the timid young man to nerve himself up to the sticking point, and boldly declare his desire to possess another half (section).[32]

The Donation Act will always be important in Oregon as the act which conveyed to individual ownership the fertile farmlands of western Oregon. Nationally it was the precursor of the Homestead Act, so long demanded on the frontier as the most fitting reward for settlers who would hold the land against all comers. In this frontier view, cultivation of land was a command of God and the Congress was merely facilitating the Lord's work in awarding land to settlers. The Oregon Donation Act was one more illustration of the pressure a frontier people could generate to convert their desires, aspirations and demands into Federal action.

---

26 Charles B. Moores, "The Donation Land Law," the Oregonian, Dec. 4, 1900.
27 Harvey Scott, "Pioneer Character in Oregon Progress," O.H.Q., XVIII (1917), 250.
28 The Oregonian, July 25, 1862.
29 Ibid., Dec. 16, 1882.
30 Robert Carleton Clark, "History of the Willamette Valley Oregon" (Chicago, 1927), pp. 394, 409.
31 Oregon Spectator, July 29, 1851.
32 Ibid., Nov. 11, 1851.

CHAPTER V

THE OREGON & CALIFORNIA GRANT

The Congress of the United States in the 19th century was the greatest land office in the world. It was constantly making and revising the policy under which a rich continental domain was being transmitted to the citizenry for development. Land legislation is never a simple matter; and the congressional agenda was always crowded with new, amendatory, and remedial public land legislation. In their inception, basic land acts were very simple: they were usually grants of land for a special purpose as part of the great expansive movement of the United States. Their application was never simple.

The Oregon & California land grant is an excellent case in point. There were larger grants to railroad corporations. There were more valuable grants, but it is doubtful if there was ever a more complicated grant. The Oregon & California grant ran a complete cycle from alienation from the public domain to revestment in that public domain. In the intervening 50 years, two corporations struggled to be declared beneficiary of its 4,200,000 acres. The two companies were absorbed by another. That company itself underwent reorganization to emerge ultimately as a part of the Southern Pacific System. The Southern Pacific became a part of the railroad empire of Edward H. Harriman. A forfeiture suit, which filled 17 volumes of testimony, came before the U.S. Supreme Court and the title to the unsold portion of the grant was revested in the United States. Once revested it became the object of an administrative struggle between two important departments of the Government.

AUTHORIZATION IN 1866

The Oregon & California land grant was one of numerous land grants authorized by the Congress in the 1860's. Its object was to aid in the construction of a railroad between Sacramento, Calif. and Portland, Oreg. By terms of the original act of 1866 the railroad was to be constructed by two companies. The California & Oregon Railroad was authorized to build through the Sacramento Valley and Siskiyou Mountains to the Oregon border. The other company was to be designated by the Oregon Legislature and was to build from Portland, Oreg., to the California border through the populated Willamette, Umpqua and Rogue River valleys.[1]

As subsidy each company was to receive 20 sections (12,800 acres) from the public domain to consist of the odd-numbered sections within a band 20 miles wide, 10 miles on each side of the right-of-way for each mile of constructed railroad. Indemnity selections were authorized 10 miles beyond the primary limits.[2]

The authorization followed an unsuccessful attempt in 1863, when the grant for the Pacific Railroad was passed, to include a grant for

[1] Stat. L., XIV, 239.
[2] Ibid., p. 240.

56227—60——4

an Oregon-California railroad.[3] In 1866, the Oregon-California grant was not considered particularly valuable. George H. Williams, an Oregon Representative in Congress, termed the land grant a matter of form rather than a grant of valuable land, as settlement in Oregon had taken up the desirable land. John Bidwell, the "prince" of California pioneers, who led the discussion on the House floor, dwelt on the nonarable features of the land and said that the grant was too small in consideration of the mountainous terrain.[4]

Oregon fear of California domination was behind the unspecified designation. Jesse Applegate, "the sage of Yoncalla" and justly famous Oregon pioneer, and W. W. Chapman, one-time surveyor-general of Oregon and Portland railroad promoter, were influential in getting an Oregon company, even though undesignated, as the grantee of the Oregon portion of the project.[5]

The Oregon Central Railroad was organized in 1866 to present itself as the recipient of the Oregon grant. It received designation from the Oregon Legislature during the 1866 session,[6] with Joseph Gaston as its principal promoter. There had been two right-of-way surveys. One by A. C. Barry ran along the west side of the Willamette Valley. The survey of S. G. Elliott was for a grade along the east side. Gaston's Oregon Central projected its road down the west side along the Barry survey and was familiarly known as the West Side Co. A rival central Oregon company was formed to build along the Elliott survey on the east side of the valley and has come down in the record as the East Side Co. (Its route was substantially that of the present mainline Southern Pacific through the Willamette Valley.)

THE DESIGNATION STRUGGLE

The East Side Co. also set out to have itself made recipient of the land grant.[7] Both roads began construction in May 1868. When the East Side Co. applied to the Secretary of the Interior for the grant, it had been preceded by the West Side Co., which had filed within the year limit prescribed by the 1866 act.

The pressure of contesting interests shifted then to the Oregon Legislature. Ben Holladay, aggressive transportation entrepreneur, was making his Northwest debut as contractor for the East Side Co. in which he was ultimately to have controlling interest. He appeared before the 1868 legislature to secure the shift of the grant designation to the East Side road. Technical defects in the incorporation papers of the West Side Co. furnished an opportunity to reopen the case. After a struggle in the lawmaking chambers at Salem, the East Side Co. was designated. There were more votes from the counties which would directly benefit from the East Side route and these votes went to Holladay's road strictly on a county basis.[8]

This action created a legal impasse. The West Side Co., which had properly filed under the granting act, had lost its designation as grantee. The East Side Co., for all its legislative designation, could not file because the deadline was passed.[9] It took congressional action to break the deadlock by an additional act, approved April 10, 1869,

[3] The Congressional Globe, 38th Cong., 1st sess., p. 2063.
[4] Ibid., 39th Cong., 1st sess., pp. 3966, 3299–3300.
[5] Scott, "History of the Oregon Country," IV, pp. 14–15.
[6] John T. Ganoe, "The History of the Oregon & California Railroad," O.H.Q., XXV (1924), 250.
[7] Ganoe, loc. cit., pp. 251–253.
[8] Ganoe, loc. cit., pp. 253–254, 257.
[9] S. Rept. No. 3 (41st Cong., 1st sess.), pp. 2–3.

written definitely in the East Side interest. It extended the time in which the application could be filed to April 10, 1870.[10] It was filed, however, in June 1869, and in October the survey for the first 60 miles was also filed.[11]

Failing in the main contest, the West Side promoters sought another grant. They proposed a railroad from Portland to Astoria via Forest Grove with a branch to McMinville. There was an attempt to have the grant extended to the head of the valley, that is, parallel to the East Side, but it was not feasible.[12] So the project was directed through the mountains of northwestern Oregon to Astoria at the mouth of the Columbia River. An act, approved May 4, 1870, granted 10 sections per mile.[13]

Debate on this act heralded the day when congressional largesse to railroads would be ended. As congressional speeches and the restrictive clauses in granting acts indicate, the congressional temper was hardening toward railroad land grants. They had begun in 1850 with a grant to the Illinois Central. They reached a climax with those to the Pacific Railroad and the Northern Pacific. By 1870 the opposition indicated that the end of the granting policy was close at hand.[14]

CHANGES IN CONGRESSIONAL ATTITUDES

In good American fashion, there had been those who would work a good thing to death. The opportunity to control vast and valuable lands through a railroad grant was not lost on promoters. They descended upon Congress literally in hordes. During debate on this Oregon Central land grant (for convenience it will be termed the "Astoria grant"), a House Member guessed that there were 90 railroad bills before the 41st Congress. He came back in a few days to say that he had been mistaken. There were 170 bills aggregating 250 million acres.[15] The pressure of these lobbyists "* * * unblushingly and persistently demanding, scarcely descending to the modesty of request * * * " was a strain on congressional generosity.

This local railroad grant in Oregon became a test of the sentiment of the Senate on railroad land grants. Allen G. Thurman, a Senator from Ohio, saw American opportunity for every man to own land threatened by land monopoly acquired through railroad land grants. Already in 1870 there were men who were fearful of the day when good, cheap land for the American people would no longer be in abundance, he recited.[16] Thurman was not against Government subsidy if it did not foster land monopoly. He suggested that the Government might sell designated lands and turn the proceeds over to railroads.[17]

THE "ACTUAL SETTLER" CLAUSE

In the House the Astoria railroad grant bill was viewed as direct violation of the homestead system. Two men were particularly keen in their attack—George W. Julian and William S. Holman, both of

---

[10] 16 Stat. 47.
[11] Ganoe, loc. cit., p. 258.
[12] Ibid., 41st Cong, 2d sess., p. 3109.
[13] 16 Stat. 94.
[14] Lewis Henry Haney, "A Congressional H story of Railways in the United States," University of Wisconsin Bulletin No. 342 (Madison, 1910), p. 20.
[15] The Congressional Globe, 41st Cong., 2d sess., p. 2362; appendix, p. 310. See Holman's speech, pp. 310-314.
[16] The Congressional Globe, 41st Cong., 2d sess., p. 966.
[17] Ibid., p. 965.

Indiana. The Astoria grant was passed, although there was one attempt to drop the land grant.[18] The sentiment against railroads did not prevent passage but it circumscribed the grant with a proviso that the land had to be sold to actual settlers at a maximum price of $2.50 per acre in units not to exceed 160 acres.[19] Indicative of a trend was a Senate amendment expressly providing for forfeiture if the clause on sale to actual settlers were not observed.[20]

Actually, these provisions had been in earlier acts. The original Oregon and California Act in 1866 contained the express provision that, if the companies did not carry out the terms, the unconveyed lands were to be revested in the United States.[21] The "actual settler" clause had been inserted in the 1869 act, which allowed the East Side Co. to obtain the original Oregon and California grant, by George W. Julian, chairman of the House Public Lands Committee and untiring watchdog of the homestead system, and passed without particular debate.[22] Supporters of this bill to extend the filing deadline for the Oregon and California grant constantly reiterated that their bill was the most closely guarded railroad bill to be presented to Congress.

The significance of the Oregon and California grant in American land grant history pivots on these "actual settler" clauses. Their flagrant violation in the 1890's was the basis of a Federal suit for recovery of the unsold lands. These provisions plus the provision in the original act that failure to comply would entail forfeiture made it possible for a Supreme Court Justice to say that the case was not of great scope in principle despite closely woven legal contention.

The 1870's were not propitious years in railroad finance. Oregon railroads passed through the same general cycle of numerous reorganizations and suspended construction. Before suspension in 1872 Ben Holladay, who controlled the East Side Co., had constructed a line 197 miles from Portland to Roseburg in the Umpqua Valley. The West Side built 47 miles to McMinnville. In 1870 the East Side Co. had been organized as the Oregon & California Railroad purchasing and consolidating the West Side holdings in 1874.[23]

Holladay was eclipsed in the Northwest after the arrival of Henry Villard in 1874, who at first represented German holders of Oregon & California bonds. Villard decided to cast his lot with the Pacific Northwest and controlled, through his holding company, the Oregon & Transcontinental, the Northern Pacific, the Oregon & California, and the Oregon Washington Railway & Navigation Co. From 1874 to 1881 while construction was suspended and various adjustments of equities were made, the Oregon & California launched a land-selling attempt. Its agents went East and to Europe to induce immigration. It offered in this early period attractive rates as low as the Government's $1.25 per acre.

The Oregon & California was completed to the California border south of Ashland, Oreg., in 1887. The grant had set 1875 as the construction deadline. It had been extended to 1880 by a special act in 1868.[24] The Oregon & California was 7 years behind in its completion. Although there were public and congressional threats of

---

18 Ibid., p. 1428. Full debate, pp. 1423–1428.
19 16 Stat. 94.
20 The Congressional Globe, 41st Cong., 2d sess., p. 1430.
21 14 Stat. 241.
22 The Congressional Globe, 41st Cong., 1st sess., p. 704.
23 *Oregon and California Railroad* v. *the U.S.*, 238 U.S. 407.
24 15 Stat. 80.

forfeitures, the belated completion forestalled them. In 1887, soon after completion, the Oregon & California was integrated with the Southern Pacific through a series of leasing agreements.

SALE OF THE GRANT LANDS

Despite the efforts to sell the land in the years before 1890, activities could hardly be described as a "land office business." By 1890, roughly one-tenth of the grant, 323,184 acres, had been patented.[25] This coincided roughly with the amount sold. The lands were not patented any great time prior to sale. Their withdrawal from entry by settlers protected the railroad and to patent them would have placed them upon the tax roll.

The salability of the grant lands was not, in the beginning, very great. In 1866, western representatives had spoken of the lands as not being particularly valuable. And for their time they were not wrong. The grant was in the mountains and hills of western Oregon, uniformally rugged, covered in many places by a heavy stand of timber, more an impediment than a crop in the 1860's. The arable lands in the Willamette, Umpqua, and Rogue Valleys had long before been settled, especially under the Donation Act. Speculators, when the prospect of the railroad was in the offing, had located land along the projected route, forcing the Oregon & California to seek locations in the indemnity limits. By mileage the Oregon & California was entitled to 4,220,000 acres.[26] There were not enough odd-numbered sections within the primary and indemnity limits to grant the road its full entitlement. In 1925, therefore, a judicial decision declared that the road was only entitled to 3,728,000 acres.[27]

In competition with Oregon & California holdings were more arable Government lands at a lower cost or no cost at all. When the mills of Michigan, Wisconsin, and Minnesota had cut the forests of the Great Lakes States, the Oregon & California lands became valuable for their crop of standing timber. They had increased by 1900 to a value variously estimated from $30 to $50 million.[28]

Before 1894 the land sales generally had been to settlers. Such sales accounted for the 300,000 acres patented by 1890. When the Southern Pacific took over the Oregon & California grant, the land department was reorganized, the timber cruised, that is, the quantity and quality of timber was estimated by experts—the cruisers—and soon a new sales policy was instituted. The 20 years from 1890–1910 were years of feverish land activity in the Northwest as Lake States timber companies hurried their agents west to buy timber land in the last and greatest timber stand on the continent. The Southern Pacific answered the new demand. In defiance of the terms of the grant, the Southern Pacific began selling, about 1894, in units well above 1,000 acres, including one sale for 45,000. The prices ranged from $5 to $40 per acre.[29]

By 1906, the Oregon & California had sold 820,000 acres. In units of less than 160 acres, 296,000 acres had been sold; in units greater than 160 acres, in other words in violation of the grant, 524,00 acres

[25] Ganoe, loc. cit., p. 338.

[26] David Maldwyn Ellis, "The Oregon California Railroad Land Grant, 1866–1945," "Pacific Northwest Quarterly, XXXIX (1948). 254. A detailed and valuable study.

[27] *U.S.* v. *Oregon California Railroad*, 8 Fed. (2d) 659.

[28] The Congressional Record, 64th Cong., 1st sess., p. 8581.

[29] "Senate Documents," 62d Cong., 1st sess., No. 27, p. 11.

has been sold. In 1903, there remained unsold in the grant 2,373,000 acres of which 2,080,000 had been patented and 293,000 remained to be patented.[30] In one set of figures Oregon & California sales are given as 813,000 acres,[31] of which 127,000 acres were sold under terms of the grant. Land sold within the acreage allowance but above the $2.50 maximum amounted to 170,000 acres. Land sold above both the acreage and price allowance amounted to 515,000 acres.

SOUTHERN PACIFIC CLOSURE

As flagrant and direct as these violations were, the Southern Pacific might have escaped censure and forfeiture had it not overplayed its hand. In 1901 the Southern Pacific was brought into the railway empire created by Edward H. Harriman at the turn of the century. Harriman was completing his reorganization of the Union Pacific when an opportunity to integrate the two systems through purchase by the Union Pacific of the Collis P. Huntington stock in the Southern Pacific presented itself.

Harriman withdrew the Oregon & California lands from sale with the explanation that the land department books needed to be examined. This was followed by announcement that effective January 1, 1903, the Oregon & California grant was closed to further sale.

Harriman had in mind holding the Oregon & California stumpage for a rise in value. The Oregonian expressed the fear that the Oregon & California would rent the lands out as a feudal estate. It even feared, in 1906, that a "compliant government" would remove the $2.50 ceiling.[32]

This closure order cost the Southern Pacific the remainder of the grant. Either Harriman did not know the temper of Oregon or did not care. An Oregonian editorial quoted Harriman as saying that the Southern Pacific was saving the Oregon & California grant for a tie reserve so that—

> * * * 20, 30, 50 years from now * * * they [posterity] shall not accuse us of wasting the resources we had at our command.[33]

For once a big corporation was vulnerable to legal attack. The sale of Oregon & California land in defiance of the law was a ready weapon to turn against the Southern Pacific when the closure aroused the communities in the land grant area. Antirailroad and antimonopoly feeling was high in these years. The Populist decade was just over and the Progressive decade was arriving when Oregon was treated to this corporate defiance of Federal law and the ingrained frontier dread of land held in mortmain.

In 1904, the Oregon & California land agent in Portland was alarmed at a notice in the Oregonian. The "actual settler" clause in the Coos Bay Wagon Road grant had been brought to public attention [34] and Oregonians were quick to see the "actual settler" clause in the Oregon & California grant as means to force the sale of the grant. The Oregon & California later charged that an executive of the Booth-Kelly Lumber Co. turned the homestead clause against them.

[30] Ibid.
[31] "House Reports," 60th Cong., 1st sess., No. 1301, p. 2.
[32] The Oregonian, Dec. 7, 1908.
[33] Ibid., Sept. 10, 1907.
[34] Ellis, loc. cit., p. 263.

He saw, of course, a supreme opportunity to wrest exceedingly valuable timberland for $2.50 per acre.

Local sentiment ran against the Oregon & California and Harriman. He was accused of blocking the development of Oregon, a high crime in any Western State, giving poor service and draining Oregon profits to deal in eastern stock manipulations.[35] Numerous suits were instituted by individuals to force the sale of Oregon & California lands. In commending these suits the Oregonian declared:

> The reign of broken pledges and greedy grab of nonresident landlords should end. Oregon aspires to a nobler destiny than striving for the pleasure and profit of these barons.[36]

In another editorial, the Oregonian advocated a graduated tax on the 5 million acres in railroad and wagon road grants as it did not approve of unearned increment on these lands going to nonresident owners.[37]

AUTHORIZATION FOR RECOVERY SUIT

The Oregon & California grant checkerboarded western Oregon, the populous portion of the State, so local feeling against the Oregon & California was widespread. It made its political appearance in a memorial, February 14, 1907, from the Oregon Legislature to Congress asking for relief from violation of the homestead clause.[38] The answer to the Oregon demand was a joint resolution introduced by the South Carolina back-country Senator, Ben Tillman. The resolution, approved April 30, 1908, authorized the Attorney General to institute suit against the Oregon & California Railroad, the Oregon Central (the Astoria grant), and the Coos Bay Wagon Road Co.[39]

The Attorney General filed the authorized suit against the Oregon & California September 24, 1908, and with it were filed 45 suits against purchasers of units of more than 1,000 acres.[40] Thus began the legal action which would end before the Supreme Court in 1915, complete with 17 bulky volumes of evidence, the greatest amount presented to the Court to that time.[41] The proceedings were not fully complete until 1925 when the accounting suit judicially determined the exact equity to which the Oregon & California was entitled.

This was not the first forfeiture threatened against the Oregon & California. In fact one forfeiture had been required by Congress. Joseph Gaston's West Side Railroad had never built beyond Forest Grove. Astoria waited for the rail connection which the Oregon Central should have furnished, but in 1882, Henry Villard, who then controlled the Oregon & California (which had taken over the Oregon Central) told Astorians that construction costs were prohibitive. Forfeiture agitation rolled into Congress and an act, approved January 31, 1885, ordered the 810,880 acres unearned by construction of the Oregon Central restored to the public domain.[42]

The main Oregon & California grant itself was threatened with forfeiture proceedings. The completion deadline for the Oregon &

[35] Scott, "History of the Oregon Country," IV, 280–282.
[36] The Oregonian, May 24, 1907.
[37] Ibid., Dec. 31, 1906.
[38] The Congressional Record, 59th Cong., 2d sess., p. 3507.
[39] Stat. L., XXXV, 571.
[40] The 45 suits were compromised in 1912 by the so-called Innocent Purchaser's Act which allowed timbermen to go to court and forfeit their title and then purchase their lands back from the United States at $2.50 per acre. Stat. L., XXXVII, 321.
[41] Ganoe, loc. cit., p. 340.
[42] Stat. L., XXIII, 296.

California was 1880; yet it was not finished until 1887. Localities along the route were naturally dissatisfied. Settlers were disconcerted because of the title uncertainty in the indemnity area until the railroad completed construction and chose its sections.[43] In 1884 a House committee urged forfeiture of that portion of grant unearned by construction on July 1, 1880.[44] There were legal arguments as to whether it was necessary for a company to earn the entire grant to earn a portion of it.[45] In the hearings, the railroad set forth the contention that cost and construction difficulty, not time, was the essence of the grant.[46] Congress seemingly accepted this view, for the attempt was dropped.

In 1908 the temper of the times had hardened against railroads. And in the *Oregon & California* case it was not now a simple failure to comply. There were certainly extenuating circumstances which in all equity could protect a grant even if construction was completed beyond the time limit. The suit before the courts in 1908 involved not noncompliance, but direct violation of the letter and the spirit of the grant; and as the Supreme Court was to reiterate in its decision the granting act was law as well as contract.

For all the legal contentions of the Oregon & California counsel, the case was rather simple. The "actual settler" clause was far too explicit to be reasoned away. If one wished, he might think of the clause as a trap set by George W. Julian to protect the homestead system. Although the Oregon & California lands were not ordained to be homesteaded, the Oregon & California snapped the trap by its unilateral action in changing the system. There were excellent reasons to alter the settler policy, but, as the Supreme Court had to assert, the recourse was congressional action, not violation of the terms of the grant.

BEFORE THE SUPREME COURT

The Government suit in 1908 sought recovery of the unsold lands' The grant was declared forfeit, in 1913, in the Federal district court for Oregon. Naturally it was taken to the Supreme Court. It was by that time no simple suit. There were five parties in the action: (1) the United States attempting to gain a forfeiture; (2) the Oregon & California Railroad fighting the forfeiture; (3) some 65 complainants asserting that a trust had been created for actual settlers; (4) certain other persons asserting that a trust had been created for any who might wish to settle; and (5) the State of Oregon which was apprehensive in the name of 18 counties that the land would be taken from the local tax roll.[47]

The Oregon & California attempted to escape the meaning of the "actual settler" clause by terming it an unenforcible covenant. The Government contended that it was a condition subsequent. Both cross-complaints and the interveners (those who asserted a trust had been created for any who might wish to settle Oregon & California lands) were maintaining that a trust had been created and were opposed to forfeiture of the grant. They desired an order forcing the

---

[43] Ellis, loc. cit., p. 258.
[44] "House Reports," 48th Cong., 1st sess., No. 2025, pp. 2-3.
[45] The Congressional Record, 48th Cong., 1st sess., pp. 4784-4801.
[46] "House Reports," 49th Cong., 1st sess., No. 931, p. 4.
[47] *Oregon and California Railroad* v. *the U.S.*, 238 U.S. 397-398, 411, 413.

company to sell or an order placing the land in the hands of receivers for sale to settlers.[48]

The Supreme Court found the "actual settler" clause an enforcible covenant, enjoined the Oregon & California from further land sales for a 6-month period and remanded the case to Congress for legislative solution.[49] It denied the cross-complainants and interveners their contention that a trust had been created.[50]

Congress responded to the Court decision with an act, approved June 9, 1916 [51] (sometimes known as the Chamberlain-Ferris Act), to provide for all the contesting interests. All Oregon & California lands, including those in the Astoria grant unsold prior to July 1, 1913, were revested in the United States. The Oregon & California was recognized as having an equity of $2.50 per acre for each acre earned by actual construction. The decision of the 1925 accounting suit found this to be 3,727,889.94 acres amounting to $9,319,724.85, of which the railroad had collected the amount of $5,242,246.50 in sale of land, timber, and interest.[52]

THE FERRIS-CHAMBERLAIN ACT

Many in Oregon expected and hoped that the Oregon & California lands would be sold for $2.50 per acre when the suit was decided. There were 14,000 to 15,000 applications filed with the Oregon & California in anticipation of such a forced sale.[53] Professional locators, including Stephen A. Douglas Puter, a leading figure of the timberland frauds of the 1900's, were advertising to locate claims for fees from $50 to $250. Nine men were so enthusiastic in their advertising that they were later convicted of misrepresentation and fraud. Congressmen asserted that Puter and his colleagues had collected $1 million in location fees.[54]

While the company was refusing to sell lands, Oregonians rushed to take up claims on the Oregon & California lands and offer the company payment. They thought that it would give them precedence if the company were forced to sell or if the land reverted to the Federal Government.[55] Many such squatters settled on Oregon & California lands in Douglas, Josephine, and Jackson Counties. An Oregonian news dispatch in 1907 tells of Salem people getting up at midnight to ride bicycles by moonlight to claims near Silver Falls east of Silverton in order to file on quartersection claims worth, by rumor, $20,000.[56] The Oregonian, however, warned in an editorial that the cases of these "actual settlers" were doubtful and thought a Government suit to force sale more appropriate.[57] During debate on the Ferris-Chamberlain Act, Oregon sentiment was decidedly in favor of the sale of the lands on the original terms [58] but the happy days when this valuable timberland could be acquired for such a pittance were over. George Chamberlain, Senator from Oregon, did not want $5,000 to $20,000

[48] Ibid., 412.
[49] Ibid., 438–439.
[50] Ibid., 436.
[51] Stat. L., XXXIX, 218.
[52] *U.S.* v. *Oregon California Railroad*, 8 Fed. (2d) 649, 660.
[53] "House Reports," 64th Cong., 1st sess., No. 623, p. 36.
[54] The Congressional Record, 64th Cong., 1st sess., p. 8584.
[55] The Oregonian, May 24, 1907.
[56] Ibid., May 29, 1907.
[57] Ibid., June 12, 1907.
[58] The Congressional Record, 64th Cong., 1st sess., p. 8589.

worth of timber sold for $400 a quarter section. Those expecting forced sale were disappointed in the Chamberlain-Ferris Act. It recognized the value in the Oregon & California lands as being the timber crop, not the land, and provided accordingly.

The acreage was to be classified as power site, timber and agricultural. Timber was to be sold by competitive bid. Agricultural land and land after the timber was logged was offered for sale at $2.50 per acre with a 3-year residence requirement.[59] There has never been a significant attempt to homestead the Oregon & California holdings.

Income from the revested lands was apportioned: (1) to pay the Oregon & California the remainder of its equity of $2.50 per acre; (2) 25 percent of the remainder to the State of Oregon for its irreducible school fund; (3) 25 percent to the counties in lieu of taxes; (4) 40 percent to the Federal reclamation fund; and (5) 10 percent to the general fund in the U.S. Treasury.[60] Under terms of this revestment, 2,891,000 acres were forfeited to the United States.[61]

Following the main decision, the Southern Pacific attempted to claim title to the timber separate from the land, but their contention was denied by the Supreme Court.[62]

The Oregon & California grant could be the prime case for a study of the public temper which fostered congressional railroad land grant legislation. The original grant passed Congress in the heyday of such grants. Its principal amendments were passed when Congress was writing restrictive clauses into the granting acts. The grant was threatened by the forfeiture agitation of the 1880's. Attempting to capitalize (figuratively and literally) on a tremendous rise in timber value, the Southern Pacific misjudged the temper of the time in the first decade of the 20th century and lost the remainder of the grant. The cycle had run full course from grant through construction to revestment, the only grant to run such full course.

They have not lost their identity. The checkerboarded O. & C. lands with their great stands of Douglas-fir timber plan an increasing role in the timber economy of western Oregon which, since the close of World War II, has become the locale of the most intense lumbering activity in the Nation.

While the long and complicated history of the administration of the O. & C. lands is an important subject in its own right, its salient points are worthy of note in passing. The O. & C. lands were brought under sustained-yield forest management by the act of August 28, 1937 (50 Stat. 874). Two years later the Coos Bay Wagon Road grant, revestment of which is outlined in a later chapter, was also brought under sustained-yield management (53 Stat. 754).

These two acts are important for three reasons. Foremost, as has been mentioned, they brought the revested lands under sustained-yield management. Secondly, a revised formula for the distribution of the revenues was provided. The revenues, now very considerable, from the O. & C. lands are distributed between the Federal Government and the counties—50 percent to be retained by the Government and 50 percent to the counties in the proportion that the assessed valuation of the lands in each county bore to the total assessed valuation of the entire grant in 1915. With respect to the Coos Bay lands,

[59] Stat. L., XXXIX, 220.
[60] Ibid., pp. 222–223.
[61] General Land Office, "Forever Timber" (Portland, n.d.), p. 6.
[62] "Senate Documents," 65th Cong., 1st sess., No. 35, p. 9.

the revenue payment is computed to be the equivalent of the taxes forgone by reason of the Federal ownership.

An additional development of administrative importance was the exchange of 482,000 acres of the so-called controverted lands which originated within the indemnity limits of the original O. & C. grant. These sections were checkerboarded through the national forests. The 1954 act required the exchange of O. & C. lands for national forest lands so that all lands within the boundaries of the national forests would be administered by the Forest Service as national forest lands while the Bureau of Land Management was given national forest lands to be administered as if they had been revested O. & C. lands (68 Stat. 270).

The 2,145,000 acres now administered by the Bureau of Land Management have an allowable timber cut of 874 million board feet. In fiscal 1960 the sale of timber from the O. & C. lands brought $32,517,157.41 into the Federal Treasury, of which $24,387,868.06 was returned to the counties. The controverted lands administered by the Forest Service grossed $4,306,623,625, as reported by the Department of the Interior in a news release on August 12, 1960.

CHAPTER VI

THE WAGON ROAD GRANTS

WAGON ROAD GRANTS IN THE MISSISSIPPI VALLEY

The Mississippi Valley was the crucible for the laws governing the disposition of the public domain. It was there that the demands arising from the aspirations of freeholders for small units of Government land at a reasonable price were granted in the act of 1820 which set the sale price of public lands at $1.25 per acre. It was from this same Mississippi Valley that arose the demand, voiced time and time again, that 160 acres should be given free to any man who would cultivate it 5 years.[1] A great political party was founded upon "free soil" and "free homesteads."

In its demands for internal improvements, the Mississippi Valley had to content itself with a compromise. Internal improvements at Federal expense—for a long generation this would be the cry of the West. It was, in large measure, denied. The South, when it passed in the 1830's to an active defense of its "peculiar institution," was implacable, on constitutional and economic grounds, to internal improvements at Federal expense. Southern leaders knew that the money to finance them would come from a high tariff, which the South viewed as a special tax on their exporting economy. The South knew the importance of principle; for though it would have benefited equally with the West by internal improvements, southern statesmen knew the implications for their society. And defense of slavery was more important than roads and canals.

However, the needs of the West of the 1840's and 1850's could not be shunted aside, even by the genius of a John C. Calhoun. The vacant public lands furnished a convenient means to subsidize internal improvements and avoid constitutional debate.

A precedent was created in the Mississippi Valley for granting public lands for railroad and wagon road construction. In the 1820's there were grants for wagon roads in Ohio and Indiana. A grant to the Illinois Central in 1850 initiated the railroad land grant policy. In 1863 there were further wagon road grants authorized in Wisconsin and Michigan. In a far different context, public lands in Oregon were granted to individuals and companies under these grants framed for the Mississippi Valley. Ironically, the wagon road grants designed to meet the needs of the Mississippi Valley were to have their most extensive application in Oregon, and largely on the arid plateaus of eastern Oregon at that.

Oregon was the one State outside the Mississippi Valley to receive land for the promotion of wagon roads. Five States—Indiana, Ohio, Wisconsin, Michigan, and Oregon—were granted a total of 3,446,188 acres for wagon road construction. Of this, 2,490,890 acres were granted for Oregon construction.[2]

---

[1] Robbins, "Our Landed Heritage," pp. 92–116.

[2] "Report of the Director of the Bureau of Land Management, 1950, Statistical Appendix," pp. 126–127. Corrected according to footnote explanations.

FIVE MILITARY WAGON ROADS IN OREGON

There were five military wagon roads constructed with land grant subsidies in Oregon: the Oregon Central Military Wagon Road (Eugene to the eastern boundary via the Middle Fork of the Willamette River); the Willamette Valley and Cascade Mountain Wagon Road (Albany to the eastern boundary via the Santiam Pass); the Dalles Military Wagon Road (The Dalles to the eastern boundary); the Coos Bay Wagon Road (Coos Bay to the Umpqua Valley) and the Corvallis and Yaquina Bay Wagon Road.

In size and subsequent importance, the first three named were the most significant. The Coos Bay road grant parallels the much larger grant to the Oregon & California Railroad in that both were reconveyed to the United States for violation of the settler's clause of their grants. The only claim to fame for the Corvallis and Yaquina Bay Wagon Road is that it is the only one of the grants which did not get taken up as a speculative holding. It was also the smallest grant and there are meager records of its construction or history.[3] Today, the balance of the grant is administered as an adjunct of the O. & C. lands.

The history of the Oregon Central, Willamette Valley, and Cascade Mountain and The Dalles roads all follow a similar pattern. The Oregon Central and the Willamette Valley and Cascade Mountain roads started in the Willamette Valley and crossed the Cascade Range, hence traversed the expanse of eastern Oregon. The Dalles road furnished a third grant running the breadth of eastern Oregon. The land grants were quickly sold by the original construction companies to land companies with sufficient capital to hold the lands off the market until about 1910 when they could be sold at a profit. All three roads, but particularly the Willamette Valley and Cascade Mountain road, were the objects of settler resentment for withholding land from settlement. Construction of all three roads was in a varying degree perfunctory, when not downright fraudulent, and Oregon settlers seized upon this as a cause for attempting forfeiture suits. The term "military road" as part of the title was a legal fiction purporting that the roads were to be built for military use. The only recorded military use of the Willamette Valley and Cascade Mountain Wagon Road was the movement of an Oregon militia company over it to join in the pursuit of Chief Joseph in 1877.[4] The land grants were all made to the State of Oregon, which in turn assigned them to the five companies. After 1874 the lands were patented directly to the companies.[5]

OREGON CENTRAL MILITARY WAGON ROAD

The first wagon road in Oregon with a land-grant subsidy was the Oregon Central Military Wagon Road which ran from Eugene, at the head of the Willamette Valley, to the eastern boundary of Oregon via the Middle Fork of the Willamette River (now the Willamette Pass where the Southern Pacific's mainline track is located), the Klamath Indian Reservation and Goose Lake Valley. The authorizing of the

[3] H. S. Bruce, "A History of the Oregon Central Military Wagon Road Company, With Reference to the Histories of Four Other Land Grant Companies in the State of Oregon" (unpublished master's thesis, University of Oregon Library, 1936), p. 68.

[4] Carroll Amundson, "History of the Willamette Valley and Cascade Mountain Wagon Road Company," University of Oregon Thesis Series No. 17 [Eugene, 1942], pp. 13–14.

[5] Stat. L., XVIII, p. 80.

grant to the State of Oregon of the alternate odd numbered sections in a band three sections wide on each side of the wagon road was enacted into law July 2, 1864.[6]

Principal promoter was B. J. Pengra, described by one writer as a man who wanted to be identified with projects of magnitude.[7] Pengra was also an ardent promoter of the Oregon Branch Pacific Railroad which would have obtained Oregon's first transcontinental railroad connection with the Central Pacific in Nevada and would have come into the Willamette Valley by the Middle Fork route used by the Oregon Central Military Road. Other backers in the venture were Eugene citizens.

The bill authorizing a grant to the State of Oregon had been introduced in the Senate in December 1863 by Oregon's Benjamin F. Harding.[8] At the same time he introduced a bill for construction of a wagon road from The Dalles to the eastern boundary, but it did not pass at that session. Pengra was in Washington to lobby for the land grant. When it was apparent that the land grant would pass, the Oregon Central Military Wagon Road Co. was formed in Eugene in April 1864. Its original capital was $30,000, later raised to $100,000. In October 1864 the Oregon Legislature assigned the grant to the Oregon Central Co.[9]

In the original bill the southern boundary of Oregon was to have been the terminus. Oregon promoters had in mind an extension to Lassen Meadows, Nev., to make connection with the Central Pacific when the overland route was completed in 1869.[10] The designation was changed in Congress to the eastern boundary.

Construction began in 1865. From Eugene to Crescent Lake, just east of the Cascade crest, a satisfactory mountain wagon road was constructed. Once on the highlands of eastern Oregon, construction became a perfunctory matter. The route went south across the Klamath Indian Reservation, then east through Goose Lake and Warner Valley to the Idaho boundary.

The Oregon Central was the only road which asked for a time extension. The others hardly needed any. The Dalles company had its certificate of completion signed 8 months after it was designated to build the road. The eastern portion of the Willamette Valley and Cascade Mountain road had been built in one season after the land grant had been made.[11] The Oregon Central was given a time extension until July 2, 1872.[12] Five years had been the construction time allotted.

The grant was sold in 1876 to the Pacific Land Co. for $125,000. It ultimately came into possession of the California & Oregon Land Co., affiliated with the Booth-Kelly Lumber Co. The grant remained pretty much intact until 1906 when the 500,000-acre portion east of the Cascades was sold to the Hunter Land Co. of Minneapolis for a reputed $700,000.[13] This company put the land up for sale in individual units.

[6] Stat. L., XIII, p. 355.

[7] Bruce, "The History of the Oregon Central Military Wagon Road Company," p. 9.

[8] The Congressional Globe, 38th Cong., 1st sess., p. 48.

[9] Bruce, "History of the Oregon Central Military Wagon Road," pp. 18, 44. Construction details, pp. 16–39.

[10] Scott, "History of the Oregon Country," III, p. 171.

[11] "Senate Executive Documents," 50th Cong., 1st sess., No. 124, p. 3. Amundson, "History of the Willamette Valley & Cascade Mountain Wagon Road Co.," pp. 13–14.

[12] Stat. L., XV, p. 338.

[13] The Oregonian, Aug. 15, 1906.

The road traversed the Klamath Indian Reservation and 110,000 acres of the grant were within the reservation. This bred a 70-year legal dispute. The tribe, of course, claimed that the United States had no right to bargain away reservation lands. When the grant was under control of the California & Oregon Land Co., a trade was arranged between the company and the tribe. The company in 1905 traded its 110,000 scattered acres, some of which had been allotted to individual Indians, for an 87,000-acre block. This block was a fine stand of ponderosa pine on Yamsey Mountain. The superintendent of the Klamath Reservation, H. G. Wilson, defended the trade as being in the Indians' benefit, although they were still not receiving compensation for lands taken from their reserve. Local Klamath observers did not see the Klamath Tribe as the beneficiary of the exchange. Frank Ira White, in a special dispatch to the Oregonian, stated that Klamath observers estimated that the land company made $2 to $3½ million on the exchange. The 87,000 acres was a valuable stand of ponderosa pine, while the traded land was pumice and jack pine thickets, worthless except for grazing.[14]

There are various estimates of the amount expended by the construction company. Naturally the company wanted to offer as large a figure as possible. At the time of its sale, a company official said it cost $125,000. A Government investigator estimated $24,-000.[15] By 1925, 875,196 acres had been patented under the terms of the grant.[16]

THE WILLAMETTE VALLEY & CASCADE MOUNTAIN WAGON ROAD CO.

A land grant was not immediately in the minds of the Linn County men who organized the Willamette Valley & Cascade Mountain Wagon Road Co. in 1864. Its principal organizers were Linn County stockmen who wanted an access road across the Cascades to reach the grazing lands of eastern Oregon. Not until financial troubles beset them did the company turn to a land grant as a means of succor. The road constructed by them was the first practical one across the Cascade Range.[17]

Originally, Lebanon had been the western terminus, but Albany, 14 miles west, was designated the western terminus although the company used a county road for its first 30 miles out from Albany.[18] From a starting point to the Deschutes River the company built in 1865 and 1866 a crude wagon road. Trees were cut out of the right-of-way, although stumps were left. Notches for the wagon wheels were cut in protruding tree roots. Some corduroy was built and some dirt bridges. It was a crude road, but for its time and place it served its purpose well. [19]

Construction costs taxed the company whose original capital was $30,000. Actually construction costs have never been determined. They have been variously estimated at $10,000, $13,000, $18,000, and $45,000.[20] By September 1866 the company officially decided to seek a land grant, a course made easy by the fact that in January 1866

[14] The Oregonian, Jan. 7, 1907. This estimate of the character of the land along the route was corroborated in an interview Feb. 21, 1951, with E. M. Bubb, Klamath Falls banker, who ran title abstracts when the grant was being sold.
[15] Bruce, "History of the Oregon Central Military Wagon Road," pp. 47–48.
[16] General Land Office, report, 1925, p. 46.
[17] Amundson, "History of the Willamette Valley & Cascade Mountain Wagon Road Co.," p. 5.
[18] Ibid., p. 6.
[19] Ibid., pp. 6–7.
[20] Ibid., p. 7; and "Senate Executive Documents," 50th Cong., 1st sess., No. 124, p. 6.

Oregon's James W. Nesmith had introduced a bill in the Senate to grant land to the State of Oregon for a military wagon road from Albany to the eastern boundary.[21] It was enacted into law July 5, 1866, and provided the standard three alternate sections per mile of construction.[22] In September 1866 the company changed its articles of incorporation to allow it to build its road to the eastern boundary; and in October it was designated by the Oregon Legislature as the beneficiary of the land grant.[23]

Its road construction from the Deschutes River to the eastern boundary was a farce. It was constructed by a small party, traveling by horseback with a light wagon following. The party moved through the country 10 or 15 miles per day, pushing down high sagebrush, blazing trees in the open timber, doing a little construction work in the bad spots, seeking suitable fords for stream crossings.[24]

From Camp Harney to Crane Creek it used a military road already in existence between Camp Harney and Winnemucca, Nev. At Crane Creek the road struck through the sagebrush highlands between the Malheur and Owyhee Rivers, using an old emigrant track part of the way. In this manner 330 miles of road was constructed in one season. The eastern portion of this road was never used. In places, later settlers were ignorant of its existence. In 1888, a Government investigator estimated that $18,000 had been spent on its construction, mostly on the western mountainous sections.[25] In total length the road was 448 miles and entitled the company to an 861,000-acre grant.

In 1870 the road, together with the land grant, was sold to T. Egerton Hogg, a railroad promoter. After numerous sales, control of the grant passed to Alexander Weill, of San Francisco, who claimed to have paid $375,000 to acquire control.[26] His main interest was, of course, the land grant and he spent his energy perfecting company titles. Title passed to the company on the strength of certificates of completion issued by the Governor of Oregon, as required in the granting act. Because there was no regular appropriation, the Governor's investigators had their expenses paid by the Willamette Valley and Cascade Mountain Wagon Road Co. Their reports disappeared from the files during a later investigation.[27]

Although the grant was for 860,000 acres, upon location of the route, 1,392,000 acres were withdrawn from settlement pending selection by the company.[28] This, naturally, irritated eastern Oregon settlers. The absentee landlord refused to sell the lands. They were leased instead. American settlers, to whom absentee landlordship and anything which hinted of land monopoly was a bitter pill, retaliated. And the company, because of the fraudulent construction, was open to attack. It had to defend its grant against a Government forfeiture suit in 1889, which it did successfully.

The grant had come under control of a French banking house, Lazard Freres, when the settlement of eastern and central Oregon attendant to railroad construction in the first decade of the 20th century renewed interest in the land grant. The grant's value had

[21] The Congressional Globe, 39th Cong., 1st sess., p. 413.
[22] Stat. L., XIV, p. 89.
[23] Amundson, "History of the Willamette Valley & Cascade Mountain Wagon Road Co.," pp. 10–11.
[24] Ibid., pp.13–14.
[25] "Senate Executive Documents," 50th Cong., 1st sess., No. 124, p. 6.
[26] Amundson, "History of the Willamette Valley and Cascade Mountain Wagon Road Company," p. 23.
[27] Ibid., pp. 24, 26.
[28] "Senate Reports," 49th Cong., 1st sess., No. 1088, pp. 3–4.

56227—60——5

by then appreciated to the point where its owners were ready to sell. It was sold in 1910 to the Oregon & Western Colonization Co. in a transaction asserted to be the largest land sale to that time. The price was given as $5 million.[29]

The Oregon & Western Colonization Co., with close connection with the James J. Hill interests, planned to promote an immigration of 100,000 persons to Oregon. The syndicate sold 660,000 acres, reserved 40,000 acres of the western portion which was heavily timbered, and in 1914 divided the remainder among members of the syndicate.[30]

THE DALLES MILITARY WAGON ROAD

The third eastern Oregon military wagon road was authorized by the usual grant to the State of Oregon in 1867. It was The Dalles Wagon Road whose construction was the most fraudulent. The Oregon Central and the Willamette Valley & Cascade Mountain Cos. built fairly satisfactory roads west of the Cascade summit. The Dalles wagon road from The Dalles to the Snake River opposite Fort Boise hardly had this to show for its 500,000-acre grant.

The grant was authorized February 22, 1867.[31] The other Oregon grants had passed without congressional debate. It was something of a sign that there was some questioning of The Dalles grant. Oregon men in Congress said that land granted had very little value. Senator George H. Williams told his colleagues that the road would be constructed through mountain and desert—

> * * * and I presume all the land that can be seen on the route of this road is not worth enough to pay for surveying it.[32]

He qualified his statement to say that the valleys might have some value. The road was being urged, according to Oregon supporters, at the behest of the military commander of the Department of the Columbia for transportation of supplies to the East.[33] It was allegedly to open communication between the Columbia at The Dalles and the mining regions of western Montana and Idaho.

Oregon Senator James W. Nesmith said the land in the grant would not sell for 10 cents an acre. Considering the grant was sold for $125,000, the Oregon representatives would seem to have been greatly mistaken in their estimates. However, in the 1860's Oregon could think of land values only in terms of the arable acres of western Oregon. Not until the wheat-growing possibilities of eastern Oregon became apparent in the 1870's did that estimate change.

There was in the House of Representatives one objection to the land grant. Francis C. LeBlond of Ohio objected to wholesale disposition of the public domain without commensurate benefit to the United States. Oregon's James H. D. Henderson was sharp in his answer that Oregon had given up asking for money for roads but thought it was entitled to ask for land.[34]

Harvey W. Scott, 40 years editor of the Oregonian, valued the lands in the grant higher than the congressional delegation. Scott

[29] Amundson, "History of the Willamette Valley & Cascade Mountain Wagon Road Company, pp. 43–44.
[30] Ibid., p. 48.
[31] Stat. L., XIV, 409.
[32] The Congressional Globe, 39th Cong., 2d sess., p. 1678.
[33] Ibid., 1st sess., p. 1870.
[34] The Congressional Globe, 39th Cong., 2d sess., p. 201.

objected to the Government's acceptance of the road until its route was straightened out.

> The route followed is about as crooked as the track of the ancient people through the wilderness—the object being to follow all the valleys of eastern Oregon and gobble up all the available lands of that region.[35]

It was built, Scott maintained, by driving an oxcart with two men walking behind with shovels. The company built the road through the middle of valleys including: The John Day, Willow Creek, Burnt River, and Malheur. One-half million acres were given to the company, which had been at no real expense. A Government estimate placed company expenditures at $6,000.[36] The true policy for the Government, Scott urged with mild sarcasm, was to extend land survey to open eastern Oregon to homesteading. "The people will then find ways enough of passing through the country." [37]

The road extended 357 miles and earned 576,000 acres. The grant was sold in 1876 to Edward Martin of San Francisco. Ultimately, it emerged from legal transactions as the property of the Eastern Oregon Land Co. The company did not, as a rule, sell land, but leased it. In wheat countries, it leased on a crop share basis. In 1910, 430,000 acres of the original grant remained. In that year, the company put its grant up for sale. It was to be sold in graded lots. In Sherman County, improved wheatland was to be sold for $25 to $40 per acre. In the John Day Valley, bottom land was priced at $75 per acre, bench land, $40 to $50; and grazing land, $6 to $10. The company also put up for sale 55,000 acres of timberland on the headwaters of the John Day River.[38]

THE CORVALLIS AND YAQUINA BAY WAGON ROAD

The smallest and least known of the Oregon wagon road grants was the Corvallis-Yaquina Bay Wagon Road grant. Details about its construction are meager. By 1925, 83,716 acres [39] had been patented by the terms of the granting act. It was the only wagon road grant which was not purchased by a land holding company. It was authorized in an act approved July 4, 1866.[40] Construction was satisfactory enough so that it did not provoke an investigation, as did the construction of the three eastern Oregon wagon roads.

The road led from Corvallis in the Willamette Valley through the Coast Range to Yaquina Bay. It was the hope of its backers that a connection with Eugene and the Oregon Central Military Wagon Road would give the Willamette Valley part of the business of supplying the mines of the interior east of the Cascades.[41]

THE COOS BAY WAGON ROAD

The last wagon road grant offered in Oregon was for construction of a 60-mile road between Roseburg, in the Umqua Valley, and Coos Bay, on the Pacific Ocean. The standard three alternate sections per mile were authorized March 3, 1869.[42] The grant was assigned to the

[35] Scott, "History of the Oregon Country," III, 99.
[36] "Senate Executive Documents," 50th Cong., 1st sess., No. 124, p. 6.
[37] Scott, "History of the Oregon Country," III, 100.
[38] The Oregonian, June 18, 1910.
[39] General Land Office, Report, 1925, p. 46.
[40] Stat. L., XIV, 86–87.
[41] Bruce, "History of the Oregon Central Military Wagon Road Co.," p. 69.
[42] Stat. L., XV, 340–341.

Coos Bay Wagon Road Co. in 1870. Construction details are lacking, but the Coos Bay Road also escaped any investigation for fraudulent construction.

The day of easy grants to railroads and wagon roads was ending in 1869. There was no concerted opposition to the Coos Bay grant, but some Congressmen had more questions to ask than they had asked about other Oregon wagon road grants. In the House of Representatives, George W. Julian, chairman of the Public Lands Committee, inserted a "settler's clause" into the grant. The amendment provided that the lands could not be sold in units larger than 160 acres at a maximum price of $2.50 per acre.[43]

In this debate Rufus Mallory, Oregon Representative, said that the land in the grant "* * * could not be sold for 1 cent an acre."[44] He did not explain why a company would be willing to acquire such valueless land. By 1925, 105,240 acres had been patented to this company.[45] A great portion of the grant was sold in 1875 against the express conditions of the "settler" clause. The grant passed to the Southern Oregon Co. in 1887. Ultimately this would be the basis for the recovery of 93,000 acres by the Federal Government.

FORFEITURE SUITS

Four of the five wagon road grants in Oregon went to the hands of land companies holding them for a rise in market value. This action, particularly by the three biggest land holding companies struck Oregon settlers at a sensitive point—fear of land monopoly. Large land holdings were anathema to these Americans. Even had the grants been honestly earned, eastern Oregon settlers would possibly not have been reconciled to their existence. With the roads a manifest fraud, local indignation was aroused.

The Willamette Valley and Cascade Mountain grant engendered the heaviest local condemnation. The Oregon Central, possibly because its land was not so desirable for settlement, did not promote so much hostility. Seemingly the Willamette Valley & Cascade Mountain Co. had been the most stubborn in refusal to sell land.

This local resentment, as it would in the American political system, found its expression in legislative halls. The Oregon Legislature demanded forfeiture of the grants for noncompliance. A citizen of Prineville, Oreg., by writing the Department of the Interior, ultimately brought on an investigation of the Willamette Valley and Cascade Mountain grant. Elisha Barnes denounced the road grant in a letter to the General Land Office in 1878. The Commissioner, stating that he would not ordinarily give credence to such unofficial statements, still recommended an investigation. Carl Schurz, at that time Secretary of the Interior, was interested in tightening land disposition procedures. He ordered an investigation of the Willamette Valley & Cascade Mountain Wagon Road Co.

W. F. Prosser was sent in 1880 to investigate. After traveling the route, except the last few miles which he gave up as an unrewarding task, Prosser reported, in summary, that the company had constructed from Albany to the Deschutes River a crude but satisfactory wagon

[43] The Congressional Globe, 40th Cong., 3d sess., p. 1890.
[44] Ibid., 40th Cong., 3d sess., p. 1820.
[45] General Land Office, Report, 1925, p. 46.

road. From the Deschutes River eastward the construction had been perfunctory to say the least.[46] The road was built by a party of men traveling 10 or 15 miles per day. Prosser estimated that, in all, $45,000 had been expended. He felt the company had earned its grant for the portion of the road crossing the mountains.[47] The chief complaint from eastern Oregon residents, Prosser found, was the company's refusal to sell the lands.

It was not altogether the lands to which the company was entitled which ostensibly delayed settlement. Actually more land was involved than that earned by construction. The Willamette Valley & Cascade Mountain Co. had earned 860,000 acres, but 1,392,000 acres were withdrawn from settlement by the General Land Office upon location of the road pending final determination and selection.[48]

The lands had been patented to the State of Oregon before being turned over to the road companies. After 1874 the lands were patented directly to the companies upon certificates of completion signed by the Governor of Oregon.[49] These certificates had all been duly signed. The eastern portion of the Willamette Valley & Cascade Mountain Wagon Road had been inspected by an agent of the Governor whose expenses were paid by the road company, as the State had no appropriation covering such work. The agent certified that the road was of "* * * such width, graduation, and bridges as to permit its regular use as a wagon road." [50]

After Prosser's report, Secretary of the Interior Carl Schurz recommended to Congress that the United States reassert ownership of the land not yet patented to the Willamette Valley & Cascade Mountain Wagon Road Co. The House Military Affairs Committee did not act upon the proposal, asserting that the subsequent owners had a clear title which could be annulled only by judicial action. The Oregon Legislature added a demand for forfeiture. In 1886, Oregon's Senator Joseph N. Dolph introduced a bill requiring forfeiture of the Oregon Central, the Willamette Valley and Cascade Mountain, and the Dalles grants. There was no action in that session.[51]

In 1887, two investigators were sent out to report upon all three roads. J. B. McNamee and G. C. Wharton traveled all three roads, taking testimony which filled 900 typewritten pages. Following their report, Congress authorized the Attorney General, on March 2, 1889, to institute suits for the recovery of the lands.[52] Three suits were immediately filed.[53] They were all dismissed in the Federal district court for Oregon.

Lack of road maintenance had been one of the sources of local complaint. The court disallowed it, ruling that construction was all the companies were bound to perform to earn land grants. The land holding companies were all able to defend themselves as "innocent purchasers in good faith." The court ruled that acceptance of the roads as completely constructed by the Governor of Oregon was conclusive proof, legally. It also ruled that the passage of the act in

[46] House Reports, 46th Cong., 3d sess., No. 332, p. 11.
[47] Ibid., p. 14.
[48] Senate Reports, 49th Cong., 1st sess., No. 1088, pp. 3–4.
[49] Stat. L., XVIII, 80.
[50] House Reports, 46th Cong., 3d sess., No. 332, p. 3.
[51] The Congressional Record, 49th Cong., 1st sess., p. 5339.
[52] Stat. L., XXV, 851.
[53] *U.S.* v. *the Dalles Military Road Company*, 40 Fed. 114; *U.S.* v. *the Oregon Central Military Road Company*, 40 Fed. 120; and *U.S.* v. *Willamette Valley and Cascade Mountain Wagon Road Company*, 42 Fed. 351.

1874 authorizing the direct patenting to the companies was an acceptance of the construction. The issuance of patents in 1882 after the Prosser investigation was a confirmatory act which would lead the purchasers of the grants to believe that their titles were good.

On these grounds all three suits were dismissed without coming to trial. The Supreme Court ordered the cases tried on their merits, but the circuit court of appeals repeated substantially the same decision as the Federal district court: the land companies were owners in good faith based upon confirmatory acts by the U.S. Government.[54]

Legally the decisions were sound, but in point of fact neither the United States nor the people of Oregon received benefit from the roads commensurate with the 2,490,890 acres granted for their construction. Even at the Government minimum of $1.25 per acre, the land subsidy amounted to more than $3 million for construction most generously estimated in the case of the three largest grants to have cost $75,000. Basically, the granting acts should have been more specific in their requirements as to construction. The laws may have been purposely general or there may have been a certain good faith that the certificate of a Governor of a sovereign State would be conclusive proof that the roads were satisfactory.

The Coos Bay Wagon Road grant was enacted when Congress was attaching more specific requirements to its grants. Violation of one such requirement allowed the United States to recover the bulk of the Coos Bay grant. George W. Julian had inserted in the Coos Bay grant a requirement that the lands could not be sold in units larger than 160 acres at a price greater than $2.50 per acre. This was broken in 1875 by the sale of the grant almost in its entirety. Its ownership came to rest in 1887 in the Southern Oregon Co.[55]

In the same 1908 resolution authorizing the suit against the Oregon & California Railroad for recovery of its 2-million-acre grant, there was authorization for a suit against the Coos Bay Wagon Road Co. upon the same grounds: violation of the settler's clause. A suit was initiated thereafter. The Government won in the lower Federal courts. In 1919, while the company was awaiting appeal to the Supreme Court, a compromise was passed in Congress. Congress authorized the dismissal of the suit and payment of $232,463.07 to the Southern Oregon Co. for its interests in the lands upon their reconveyance to the United States.[56] The money represented the $2.50 per acre maximum which Congress intended the company should derive from its grant. Ninety-three thousand acres in Douglas and Coos Counties were reconveyed to the United States. These lands are at present administered under the basic arrangement provided in the reconveyance of the Oregon and California lands by the Bureau of Land management.

OREGON CENTRAL GRANT AND THE KLAMATH INDIANS

Another thread in the legal skein cost the United States $5 million. As has been recited, 110,000 acres of the Oregon Central grant were within the Klamath Indian Reservation. After the general forfeiture attempt failed, the United States, on behalf of the Klamaths, sought

[54] 140 U.S. 600; 49 Fed. 500; 51 Fed. 638; 55 Fed. 712.
[55] *Southern Oregon Company* v. *the U.S.*, 241 Fed. 16.
[56] 40 Stat. 1179–1180.

to revoke the patents for land within the reservation. The Government could not recover the land. A 1904 Supreme Court decision confirmed the wagon road grant within the reservation.[57] Congress in 1905 and 1906 authorized and confirmed the trade of 110,000 acres for 87,000 acres in one block of reservation land.[58] For all this the Klamaths received no compensation. In 1938, after numerous court trials and special congressional legislation, the Klamath Tribe won a $5 million judgment in the Supreme Court as compensation for the land and timber of the 87,000-acre unit.[59]

In acts from 1864 to 1869 Congress appropriated grants for five wagon roads in Oregon which ultimately alienated 2½ million acres from the public domain, involved the United States in numerous lawsuits, and cost $5 million to adjust a grant within the Klamath Reservation. It is difficult to see that any benefit was conferred commensurate with this expense. Seemingly, the only road which served a real need was the mountain portion of the Willamette Valley and Cascade Mountain Road and possibly the Coos Bay and Corvallis-Yaquina Bay Roads.

[57] *U.S.* v. *California & Oregon Land Co.*, 192 U.S. 357.
[58] 33 Stat. L. 1033; 34 Stat. 368.
[59] *U.S.* v. *Klamath and Moadoc* [*Modoc*] *Tribes of Indians*, 304 U.S. 119. The exact amount is $5,313,347.32.

CHAPTER VII

GRANT TO THE STATE OF OREGON

Together with individuals and companies the State of Oregon has been a major recipient of public lands from the United States. Oregon received 4,309,435 acres [1] from the Federal Government as its "dowry" upon admission to the Union, in keeping with the standard practice of giving to the States created from the public domain a generous patrimony with which to begin functioning as sovereign States. Practically all of the Oregon grant was devoted to the support of education. The swamplands granted to Oregon were the only significant exception, and in their case 10 percent of the revenue from their sale went into the irreducible school fund.[2]

A feeling exists that Oregon may have wasted its patrimony by unwise sale. This may be due to envy, among some Oregonians, of the State of Washington which supposedly made wiser use of its grant.

Except for some rather valueless grazing land in eastern Oregon and one small tract of State-owned timber, Oregon has sold its grant. Oregon's stand of timber was the largest per acre in the Nation; yet the State is not a significant owner of timberlands. Washington was admitted to the Union in 1889 when the value of timberland was much more apparent, and Washington carefully guarded its school lands for their potential worth. Oregon had something of the same opportunity except there was a 30-year precedent for the State to sell its lands for immediate profit. Oregon did not realize the potential value of its grant for two reasons: Prior settlement, under the Donation Act, and slowness of survey, for settlers could use their preemption right to settle unsurveyed land, denying the best agricultural lands to the State. The first generation of Oregon settlers thought of land value solely in terms of arable farmland. Oregon timberland did not become valuable until after 1890, and then the precedent for immediate sale of State land was too well ingrained to be readily changed. The State lands were sold when sparse settlement and a vast acreage of unoccupied land placed a definite ceiling on their value. Actually, the $1.25 and $2.50 per acre which the State received for various grants, until the timber boom of 1900–1910, were good prices for the time.

STATE LANDS IN THE TIMBER BOOM

The purchase of idemnity school land became a major means of acquiring holdings during the timber-buying boom of 1890–1910. Between 1898 and 1905, 1,381,327 acres of the State lands were sold.

[1] Report of the Director of the Bureau of Land Management, 1950 Statistical Appendix, p. 126, with corrections according to explanations, except that Oregon did not receive the salt springs grant. Wagon road grants and Carey Act lands are not treated essentially as grants to the State of Oregon. The standard monograph is Mathias Nordberg, "Federal Grants to the States with Special Reference to Minnesota," "University of Minnesota Studies in Social Science," No. 2 (Minneapolis, 1915).

[2] This chapter is not intended to be a complete study on the State lands. As the vast majority of Oregon lands were dedicated to school support, Ray Norman Hawk, "A History of the Irreducible School Fund in Oregon" (unpublished doctoral dissertation, University of Oregon Library, 1949), especially chs. IV–VI, is such a study.

This rapid sale cost the State of Oregon an opportunity to acquire blocks of timberland when the national forests were created. It could have traded school sections within the forests for timberland outside the forests. One State land agent urged such action,[3] but promptness, the essence of the action, was not forthcoming. Although the State may have lost out in selling its timberlands, those lands did go onto the tax rolls of local units of government and their passage from State ownership cannot be assumed to be a total loss to the public good.

The merging of selection and sale as essentially a single operation in the disposition of the State grants is a characteristic which led to confusion, shady practices, and in some instances to uncertainty of title. This merging of selection and sale was prevalent in the disposition of school indemnity lands and the swamplands. If a section designated as part of the school grant was already occupied upon survey, or was within a forest or Indian reservation, it was, of course, lost to the State of Oregon, made up by the Federal Government which allowed the State to select "lieu" or "indemnity lands." The selection of the "lieu" land was more or less left up to individuals in this manner: A person desiring to purchase a piece of land from the State would designate the base section (or fraction) and request the State to select the parcel which the individual wished as the "lieu" land. The State upon receipt of a down payment would issue a certificate of sale and request the land from the Federal Government. When the State received its patent, it collected the remainder of the sale price from the individual and in turn issued him a deed.

The indemnity lands were important in the disposition of the public domain in Oregon, particularly in the disposition of timberland. Because of prior settlement, slow surveys, and the acreage covered by forest and Indian reservations and the mineral claims, Oregon lost more base, that is, the 16th and 36th sections, than any other State.[4]

Oregon law limited the sale of land to 320 acres to a settler and 160 acres to a nonsettler.[5] However, the certificates of sale which the State issued before actually conveying the title were transferable and made the limitations a dead letter.[6] There were good reasons for buying from the State. During much of the timber boom the State price for land was $1.25 per acre, which was one-half the $2.50 per acre required under the Timber and Stone Act.

Records of early State land transactions were kept at a local level and were lost; land for which the State had no claim was sold. There are no records of sales prior to 1870, and those between 1870 and 1878 are incomplete and inaccurate.[7] And in one instance, certificates of sales were the objects of a large-scale forgery scheme.

Part of this poor recordkeeping may have come from the eagerness of the State to sell its land or the eagerness of purchasers to buy. Settlers with a valid preemption right were authorized to purchase vacant school sections for $1.25.[8] A State preemption system was instituted for the internal improvement grant. A law of 1860 authorized settlers to preempt not less than 40 acres nor more than 320

---

[3] Hawk, "A History of the Irreducible School Fund in Oregon," p. 156; [Oregon] State land agent, First Biennial Report, 1896, p. 18.
[4] F. G. Young, "Financial History of the State of Oregon," O.H.Q., XI (1910), 123.
[5] General Laws of Oregon, 1878, p. 42.
[6] Hawk, "A History of the Irreducible School Fund in Oregon," p. 112.
[7] Ray O. Wolf, "A History of Oregon School Lands, 1849–1900" (unpublished master's thesis in University of Oregon Library, 1940), p. 74.
[8] General Laws of Oregon, 1866, p. 28.

acres of the internal improvement grant. The price was $1.25 per acre with only interest paid until surveys were complete, when the sale price was to be turned over a State locating agent.[9]

Oregon settlers and American landowners in general were sensitive to blots on land titles. Seemingly some Oregon settlers lived in fear that in some manner the laws would be perverted to deny honest hard-working settlers full title to their homesteads. In retrospect, however, it would seem that settlers in their desire to gain a right to land put themselves in legal situations in which technicalities could cloud their legal titles. The operation of the State preemption system was certainly a case in point. Settlers agreed to buy unsurveyed land when it was surveyed. In Baker County seemingly there were complications to this system. When the time came to pay, some settlers did not have the cash. In fear that they would lose their homesteads, they held angry meetings. At one of these meetings a long list of resolutions was passed, one of which declared—

> * * * that anyone who is base enough to take advantage of our present inability to comply strictly with the requirements of the law will be summarily dealt with.[10]

This was, of course, one more instance of the feeling voiced time and time again on the frontier that land should belong to those who would work it, irrespective of legal technicality.

LAND PROVISIONS OF THE ADMISSION ACT

The lands granted Oregon were largely provided for in the Admission Act of 1859, but three important ones were distinct grants. The 500,000-acre internal improvement grant was given under the terms of an act of 1841.[11] In 1850, Congress had granted the swamp and overflow lands within their borders to the public land States. There were 13 such States; in 1860 the act's provisions were extended to Minnesota and Oregon.[12] Two years later a land subsidy for higher education was added by terms of the Morrill Act which granted each State 30,000 acres for each Representative and Senator in the Congress for the support of an agricultural college. Oregon with one Representative and two Senators received the minimum of 90,000 acres.

The Admission Act itself contained grants which had their precedent in the Mississippi Valley. Some of the grants had been anticipated in the Oregon Territorial Act of 1848 which had reserved the 16th and 36th sections in each township for the support of common schools.[13] Two townships (46,080 acres) were also reserved for a university by the Donation Act.[14] In the Admission Act, 12 salt springs were granted with contiguous lands totaling 46,080 acres as well as the tidelands and 5 percent of the revenue from the sale of public lands in Oregon.[15] In all, Oregon has received as its grant from the United States for:

	Acres
Common schools	3, 399, 360
Other schools	136, 165
Internal improvements	500, 000
Swamplands	286, 108
Public buildings	[1] 6, 400

[1] Report of the Director of the Bureau of Land Management, 1950, Statistical Appendix, p. 126.

[9] Ibid., 1860, pp. 55–56.
[10] The Oregonian, Feb. 22, 1871.
[11] Stat. L., V, 455.
[12] Stat. L., XII. 3.
[13] Ibid., IX, 330.
[14] Ibid., 499.
[15] Ibid., XI, 383–384.

Oregon did not act in haste to take possession of its grant. Almost a decade passed before the State took concerted action. The citizens did not consider vacant lands particularly valuable.[16] The first generation of Oregon settlers thought of desirable arable land as the valley land of western Oregon. This generation did not think in terms of timberland or irrigable land. In 1864 the legislature asked Congress to grant the unsurveyed lands to the State for internal improvements. It did not consider that they would be a valuable gift.[17]

To Lafayette Grover, Governor from 1868 to 1876, securing the State's grant was the keynote of his administration.[18] By that time the salt springs grant had been lost by default and the swamp grant nearly so. From Grover's time the State was conscious of the value of its grant and ready to claim all lands which were due the State.

Oregon has not retained a significant portion of its grant. Some 700,000 acres of grazing land remain in eastern Oregon. It is not a significant owner of timberlands.[19] Retrospect points to the wisdom of holding the State lands for the increase in value which came with a phenomenal rise in timber value and a general advance with the increase in the State's population. The State lands were sold under a prevailing sentiment that the best benefit would accrue to the State by their immediate sale for individual development. They were sold in competition with the millions of acres of Federal lands readily available; the lands of the State were not valued for their potential worth; much of the land was sold when the population was sparse and the vacant land plentiful.[20]

SCHOOL LANDS

The school lands grant to Oregon was embodied in the Oregon Territorial Act of 1848. It provided that sections 16 and 36 in each township were to be reserved to the Territory for the support of common schools.[21] The grant of the 16th section was in the Jeffersonian precedent that public education was the sine qua non of a democratic republic's existence. The amount of land reserved for common schools was doubled in the Oregon Territoral Act, the first law to provide the additional 36th section for a territory although California was the first State to receive a double portion.[22]

As has been stated, Oregon lost more school sections because of prior settlement, Government reservations and mineral rights than any other State. The Donation Act land claims in the Willamette, Umpqua and Rogue Valleys had a prior claim to these desirable lands.

---

16 Young, loc. cit., X (1909), 372.

17 Ibid., quoting Oregon "Special Laws," 1864, pp. 11–12.

18 Ibid., p. 377.

19 Bureau of Corporations, "The Lumber Industry" (Washington, 1913), I, 252.

20 Young, loc. cit., XI (1910), 131–132.

21 Stat. L., IX, 330.

22 J. Quinn Thorton, prominent leader in the provisional government, late in life claimed credit for securing the additional 36th school section. In 1848 Thorton was an unofficial delegate from the provisional government to Congress to promote territorial status. In 1873, he claimed to have written the Oregon Territorial Act including the double school grant. "I felt a vehement desire," he wrote, "to so multiply, in Oregon, the springs of knowledge that pure streams might then flow out to water all the land, and to gladden unborn generations thirsting for literary and scientific knowledge. * * * And I will frankly admit that when to this section of the public lands [the 16th] the 36th was added * * * the thought that Providence had permitted me to be the instrument of conferring so great a boon upon posterity, filled my heart with emotions as pure as can be experienced by man."

Thorton must have been the victim of self-delusion. Frances Fuller Victor has shown convincingly that Thorton could not have been in Washington when the bill was drafted. For Thorton's statement, see Oregon Pioneer Association, "Transactions," 1873, pp. 88, 95. For Victor's contention see O.H.Q., I (1899), 148.

Indemnity was offered the State government in "lieu" of these lost sections (or fraction of sections). The indemnity lands were not only sold through a complicated process, but became a basis for several species of graft. The State did not select its indemnity lands. Their selection and sale were merged. Individuals selected lands which they purchased from the State and then waited for the State to acquire title before transferring it to them.

School "base," the original 16th and 36th sections in each township, was used as a means of acquiring land from the public domain. An Oregon law in 1887 required a purchaser of indemnity land to furnish legal description of the base tract upon which the indemnity was being claimed.[23] This information was kept in the hands of men with connections in the office of the secretary of the State land board. These traffickers sold their base designations at a per acre price ranging from $1 to $2.50.[24]

Applicants for State indemnity lands paid $250,000 for 133,564 acres of base designations from three Oregon Indian reservations.[25] There was even a more complicated maneuver to create "base." Men with knowledge of the administrative procedure of the General Land Office would have school sections declared mineral in character by an affidavit. This allowed the State to make a tentative "lieu" selection, which would then be sold. The "base" broker would take his fee for providing "base" and disappear from the scene. There were three parties to this transaction: the purchaser, the State of Oregon, and the United States. Had the mineral allegations been in good faith, accounts might have balanced, but the affirmations of mineral character were not made in good faith. When that fact was finally uncovered, one of the three parties would suffer. It was the State of Oregon which had to make good from its other lands the indemnity lands it had sold upon fictitious "base." In 1896 a conscientious State Land Agent estimated that 20,000 to 30,000 acres of the State land would be needed to make good indemnity selections made upon fictitious "base." [26] Only 26,000 acres of indemnity land based upon 60,000 acres of allegedly mineral sections were confirmed by the Federal Government.[27]

School indemnity lands were a favorite means of blocking out tracts of timber land in the timber buying boom of 1890–1910. The search for "base" was one of the features of this boom as timber speculators gathered together units of timber land. Two sizable Oregon timber holdings were based upon the school lands.[28] State indemnity lands were desirable because they cost $1.25 per acre, the price for the commuted homestead, a homestead which was purchased after 14 months' occupancy, but only half as much as land bought under the Timber and Stone Act. The price of "base" sometimes drove the land to $4 per acre,[29] but seemingly purchasers did not care. The actual loser was the State of Oregon which might just as well have had the difference.

School sections were the objects of speculative solicitude in northeastern Oregon in the early 1900's. When news leaked out that

[23] General Laws of Oregon, 1887, p. 74.
[24] [Oregon] State Land Agent, First Biennial Report, 1896, pp. 3–4.
[25] Ibid., p. 6.
[26] Ibid., pp. 11–12.
[27] [Oregon] State Land Agent, First Biennial Report, 1896, p. 10.
[28] Bureau of Corporations, Lumber Industry, I, 252.
[29] [Oregon] State Land Agent, First Biennial Report, 1896, p. 6.

forest reserves were contemplated in northeastern Oregon, there was a pressure to buy school sections within the anticipated boundaries.[30] By operation of the Forest Lieu Act of 1897, these school sections within a reserve could be traded for sections outside the reserve. Relatively worthless rocky sections of northeastern Oregon could then be traded for timbered sections blocked together elsewhere.

The office of State land agent was created in 1895 to select the land owing to the State of Oregon, to ascertain the loss of land due to prior settlement, and to select in its place the best timberlands available.[31] The indemnity lands were withdrawn from sale for 2 years and their price raised to $2.50 per acre, although it was returned in 1899 to $1.25.[32] To curtail the traffic in "base," the records of the State land board were made readily accessible.[33] A 1903 act halted the selling of indemnity lands for mineral sections until their mineral character had been determined by the General Land Office. This same law proclaimed that no priority of right of purchase would obtain to the disclosure of deficits for which the State might have an indemnity right. "All information * * * shall be deemed purely voluntary and for the benefit of the school fund." [34] The State never took advantage of its indemnity selections to acquire blocks of timberland.

THE INTERNAL IMPROVEMENT GRANT

By an act of 1841 each State when admitted to the Union was granted 500,000 acres for internal improvements. In Oregon the grant was selected principally in Baker, Union, and Umatilla Counties in northeastern Oregon. It was ultimately sold at $1.25 in currency to actual settlers and in gold coin to others. By congressional resolution in 1871 the proceeds from the grant were diverted to the common school fund.[35]

THE UNIVERSITY GRANT

The Donation Act of 1850 reserved two townships for the support of a territorial university. Both townships were to be west of the Cascade Mountains, one north and one south of the Columbia River.[36] In the Admission Act for Oregon in 1859, 72 sections were granted for a State university. The selections were to be made by the Governor and approved by the surveyor-general of Oregon.

Selection and sale were begun before statehood. The first selections were made in 1853, and approximately $9,000 worth of land was sold at public auction in 1855–56. Selections were made for the entire grant, but the procedure necessary to perfect title was not carried out. The lands were originally located in the river bottom of the Willamette and its tributaries, but this failure to perfect title forced an ultimate selection of less desirable lands.[37] A $4 per acre minimum halted early sales.

---

[30] [Oregon] State Land Board, Biennial Report, 1905, pp. 8–9.
[31] General Laws of Oregon, 1895, p. 7.
[32] Ibid.
[33] Ibid.
[34] Ibid., 1903, p. 308.
[35] Stat. L., XVI, 595.
[36] Ibid., IX, 499.
[37] Young, loc. cit., X (1909), 373–374.

THE AGRICULTURAL COLLEGE GRANT

The 90,000 acres allotted Oregon under the Morrill Act were located in one tract in Klamath and Lake Counties. The legislature in 1868 appointed a special committee to make the selections. At the time, the area was remote from settlement and not subject to entry. Congress approved the selections in 1872 with the stipulation that their minimum sale price be $2.50.[38]

SWAMP LANDS

The Congress granted, in 1850, the swamp and overflow lands within their borders to the public land States. The States turned these lands over to private individuals who, in the name of the States, pushed the definition of swampland as far as it could be taken, to encompass an acreage three times greater than the highest figure anticipated by Congress. Like other land legislation which governed the disposition of the public domain in the Far West, the swamp grant rose from conditions in the Mississippi Valley.

Oregon swamplands were not in well-watered western Oregon, but along the lake margins of the large lakes of southeastern and south central Oregon. Harold Hathaway Dunham in "Government Handout" records an instance where the General Land Office suspected fraud because it had discovered two adjoining entries, one a swampland selection and the other a Desert Land Act claim.[39] Whether or not there was fraud, it would have been possible in parts of eastern Oregon for a swamp and desert claim to adjoin.

The swamp grant was extended to Minnesota and Oregon in 1860[40] to bring 15 States under its terms. Oregon has received 286,108 acres.[41] Although the swamplands were granted in 1860, Oregon did not bestir itself about them until 1870 when it passed an act to arrange for their selection and sale.[42]

The Department of the Interior recognized two methods of swampland selection: (1) selection from the survey plats or (2) selection by a State agent. The selections under the Oregon law of 1870 were not recognized by the Interior Department because the law failed to stipulate the mode of selection. In 1874 the legislature complied with the Federal request for a better designation of selection. The swamplands were sold under this 1870 act at $1 per acre gold coin with 20 percent as a down payment and three hay crops within 10 years to constitute reclamation.[43] The State on this down payment issued a certificate of sale and had to await its own ability to give patent to the purchaser. Under the 1870 law 266,600 acres were selected by State agents, but the selections were not recognized.

Under the 1870 act one individual received the bulk of the swamp. He was H. C. "Hen" Owens, cited by one writer as an agent for a foreign syndicate.[44] By 1882 he had made a down payment on 225,907 acres of swampland.[45] The State accepted the down payment on more

[38] Stat. L., XVII, 217.
[39] Harold Hathaway Dunham, Government Handout: A Study in the Administration of Public Lands, 1875–91 (New York, 1941), p. 288.
[40] Stat. L., XII, 3.
[41] Report of the Director of the Bureau of Land Management, 1950, Statistical Appendix, p. 126.
[42] General Laws of Oregon, 1870, p. 55.
[43] Ibid.
[44] Young, loc. cit., XI (1910), 158.
[45] [Oregon] State Land Board, Biennial Report, 1884, p. 57.

swampland than it delivered. This resulted from an interpretation of a law of 1878 which raised the purchase of the swamplands to $2.50 per acre in lots larger than 320 acres. However, the State land board honored applications made under the 1870 law even though money had not been paid down.[46] In 1887 the legislature ordered the return of down payments made after 1879.

Hubert Howe Bancroft in his "History of Oregon" asserts that members of the legislature active in the passage of the 1870 Swamp Act had their maps and notices all prepared to file upon the Governor's signature. He tells that one eager applicant called at the Governor's office in the evening to see if the Governor had signed the bill; he was told that he had not and would not that evening. He left planning to be present the first moment in the morning. In the meantime the Governor did sign the bill and another eager but more persistent applicant filed his application.[47]

Purchase or attempted purchase in large acreages was a feature of the swampland disposition. Four hundred eighty-five thousand seven hundred and seventy-seven acres were sold to one man, but the sale was repudiated.[48] As large as were the acquisitions under the swamp sales, they were almost 10 times larger by report. Reports may have been exaggerated by Western dread of that ogre—land monopoly. The editor of the Sacramento Union saw a threat to the Republic in Oregon swamp acquisition.

> This wholesale land grabbing—

he wrote—

> is the bane of the Republic. It is the incipient step to the elevation of a patrician order in society, from which the Republican freeman has nothing to hope.[49]

Acquisition of large blocks of land by individuals was viewed "with alarm" upon the frontier. Oregon settlers had a fear, justified by just enough cases to keep it alive, that their improved holdings might fall into the hands of speculators through the machinations of the "swamp angels." The Jacksonville Sentinel, in 1871, warned that swampland purchasers might try to get a refund on their $1 per acre purchase price. This same paper expressed a fear that settlers might lose their improved claims and asserted that it would be better for the State to lose the swampy margins of the Klamath and Goose Lakes than for settlers to lose their claims.[50]

Some people did not like the fact that men by a 20-percent downpayment controlled the land for years.[51] The editor of the Oregonian attacked the Democrats who had passed the 1870 Swamp Act. He feared it would block settlement and Harvey W. Scott was categorically against anything which would block Oregon settlement. After this attack by the leading Republican paper, a Republican's swamp grant was contested. The Democrats were quoted as saying:

> * * * since the Republicans have made a fuss about it [the swamplands] no d—d Republican shall have a snoot full. If the galled jade of democracy is wincing already, it will find its withers terribly wrung before we get through exposing the iniquities of its legislation and the practices of its spoilsmen.[52]

---

[46] Young, loc. cit., XI (1910), 156–159.
[47] Bancroft, Works, XXX, 67 n.
[48] Young, loc. cit., XI (1910), 160–161.
[49] Sacramento Daily Union, Jan. 15, 1872.
[50] Reprinted in The Oregonian, Nov. 29, 1871.
[51] The Oregonian, Nov. 18, 1886.
[52] Ibid., Jan. 12, 1872.

There were other practices to alienate popular sentiment. The selection of swampland was also merged with its purchase. Selection agents were in fact its purchasers, and it was the custom at one time to pay a selection fee from the 20-percent downpayment. One individual rendered a selection fee bill which just covered the 20 percent on 4,400 acres of swampland.[53] One homesteader with patented land paid a swamp locator $200 for the claimant's deed which was not in force, for the land had not been approved by the General Land Office,[54] a good illustration of Western fear of adverse claims to land and the willingness of settlers to buy off legal entanglements.

Oregon pushed its claim for every possible acre of swampland. In 1903–4 the General Land Office and the Secretary of the Interior denied a claim to 92,378 acres of swampland on the Klamath Indian Reservation. The State attempted to claim swamplands within the reservation because the grant to Oregon in 1860 was a grant in praesenti, that is, the title to all swamplands passed immediately to Oregon even though title to specific tracts was not confirmed. Oregon contended that its right antedated the Indian right because the reservation was not created until 1864, but the Secretary of the Interior refused to accept this interpretation.[55]

Swampland selections and sale were largely confined to the major lakes of south central and southeastern Oregon: upper and lower Klamath Lakes (the lower Klamath was partially in California and has been drained for farming); Tule Lake (also partially in California and now reclaimed as the most productive portion of the Bureau of Reclamation's Klamath project); Goose Lake (also partially in California); Warner Lakes; Harney and Malheur Lakes. The swamplands were largely converted into meadowlands for cattle ranches.

There are numerous allegations of fraud in the swampland selections. And figures do bear out the charge that a great number of acres were not accepted by the General Land Office as swampland. In one instance, 33,000 acres in the Klamath country was found, on close investigation, to be dry land. The special Federal investigator found that his predecessor had been physically incapacitated at the time he had sworn that he had viewed the tracts. The original Federal agent had a written agreement to receive a large sum from the claimant for certifying the tracts as swampy.[56] By 1888, 233,000 acres had been claimed as swamplands. The General Land Office found 111,000 acres dry.[57]

The State did not always receive cash for the swamplands. It accepted instead warrants issued for construction projects of dubious worth. The warrants were issued in anticipation of the sale of swamplands. H. C. Owens made a 20-percent downpayment on 55,185 acres amounting to $11,037.07 during the 1880's with such warrants which bore 10 percent interest and consumed the sale price from 14,000 acres per year for interest.[58] These warrants were receivable as payment for swampland until 1878.

---

[53] Wolf, "A History of Oregon School Lands, 1849–1900," p. 89.

[54] The Oregonian, Apr. 15, 1873.

[55] [Oregon] State Land Board, Biennial Report, 1905, pp. 11–17.

[56] "Senate Executive Documents," 50th Cong., 1st sess., No. 161, p. 1; General Land Office, Report, 1886, p. 41.

[57] General Land Office, Report, 1888, p. 44.

[58] [Oregon] State Land Board, Biennial Report, 1880, p. 27; ibid., 1886, p. iv.

MINOR GRANTS

Oregon was granted 6,400 acres as subsidy for public buildings. These lands were selected and sold without incident. Oregon lost its salt springs grant. In the Mississippi Valley the salt springs were essential to life. Their possession was reserved to the Federal Government which conveyed some of them to the States as desirable portions of the State land grant. There were, of course, no salt springs in Oregon, although it is conceivable that the State might have claimed the 46,080 acres tendered in the salt springs grant without having to offer absolute proof. The salt springs had to be selected within 1 year of a State's admission. The time limit proved too short and Congress in 1860 granted an extension of 3 years.[59] In 1870, the springs had not been selected and the Oregon Legislature asked for another extension; [60] but no action was taken.

The State was also granted the tidelands. By 1904, an estimated 18,000 acres had been turned over to Oregon which had received $40,000 by their sale.[61] Oregon has also received, according to the terms of the Admission Act, 5 percent of the money received from the sale of the U.S. public lands within its borders.

Oregon has not retained a significant portion of its grant, but has sold the grant lands generally for $1.25 and $2.50 per acre. In retrospect, it might be argued that the State should have held its lands, particularly those which would be valuable as timberlands, but the concepts of the times, strongly in favor of individual ownership and development, did not favor such holdings. The price received for State lands would seem adequate in view of sparsity of settlement and availability of land.

However, the State lands were subject to a host of shady practices, particularly in the efforts to create base from which to select indemnity lands. The merging of selection and sale, while it undoubtedly hastened the transfer of land to individuals, created confusion and an opportunity for shady practices.

---

[59] Stat. L., XII, 124.

[60] "House Miscellaneous Documents," 41st Cong., 3d sess., No. 20.

[61] Charles MacC. Snow, "A History of Oregon Land Grants," (unpublished bachelor's thesis, University of Oregon Library, 1909), p. 37.

CHAPTER VIII

THE DISPOSITION OF TIMBERLANDS

EARLY LACK OF VALUE

In retrospect it is odd that the first generation of Americans in Oregon did not consider their timber valuable. Even such a well-informed observer as Harvey W. Scott, famous editor of the Oregonian and vigorous exponent of the development of Oregon, did not recognize the potential value of Oregon timber. In the 1870's, 20 years before the first stirrings of interest and 30 years before the boom in timberland, he wrote:

> It is not right to humbug people abroad with the idea that these railway lands are valuable [the Oregon & California Railroad grant]. They are simply ordinary mountain lands, covered for the most part with immense forests of fir trees situated where timber is no object, expensive to open [for agriculture] and only second or third rate when open.[1]

Three forces brought value to the hitherto unvalued timberlands of Oregon: the depletion of the timber stand in the Great Lakes States; anticipation of a timber famine fostered by alarmed conservationists and the accelerated creation of national forests as part of the conservation movement.

The immensity of the forests to which Harvey W. Scott referred is to be seen in the statistics. In 1952, after 60 years of cutting, the Pacific Northwest (Oregon, Washington, Idaho, and western Montana) had 97 million acres of timberland, 45 percent of the national total, with 900 billion board feet of sawtimber.[2] Of these States, Oregon had the highest percentage of timberland. Forty-six percent of Oregon's 61 million acres was classified as forest land.[3] Not only that but its per acre yield was the highest in the Nation.[4] In 1952 Oregon had 48 percent of the sawtimber in the Pacific Northwest.

Oregon's commercial forest, embracing 26 million acres, gives it the highest percentage of forest land of any State except for newly admitted Alaska. In western Oregon there are over 14,500,000 acres carrying 337 billion board feet, mainly the lordly Douglas-fir. Eastern Oregon's 11,400,000 timbered acres carry 96.5 billion board feet, mainly the stately ponderosa pine.[5]

Western Oregon was once five-sixths timberland. On the mountains and hills of western Oregon the heavy rains from the Pacific fall to promote the growth of the Douglas-fir, the predominant species. The Douglas-fir is not only a large tree itself, but it grows thickly.

East of the Cascades the ponderosa pine is predominant. The ponderosa pine grows on the semiarid plateaus and volcanic buttes of the mountains of eastern Oregon in several large blocks of forest.

[1] The Oregonian, June 26, 1873.

[2] "Timber Resources for America's Future," U.S. Forest Service, Department of Agriculture, Washington, 1958. Forest Reserves Report No. 14. Hereafter cited as "Timber Resources."

[3] National Resources Committee, "Forest Resources of the Pacific Northwest" (Washington, 1938), p. 10. Hereafter cited as "Forest Resources of the Pacific Northwest."

[4] John Ise, "The United States Forest Policy" (New Haven, 1921), p. 321.

[5] "Timber Resources."

It takes longer to mature than the Douglas fir, is much more sparse but infinitely easier to log. The principal ponderosa stand is in Klamath and western Lake Counties and in the Ochocho Forest of Crook County.

PRIVATE OWNERSHIP OF TIMBER

The latest inventory of America's timber resources was published in 1958 reflecting the situation as it existed in 1952. Oregon's position in that study is summarized in the following tables:

Commercial forest land

[Millions of acres]

	Private	Government						Total Government	Grand total
		State and local	Federal						
			National forests	Bureau of Land Management	Other	Total Federal			
Western Oregon	6.6	0.9	4.7	2.3		7.0		7.9	14.5
Eastern Oregon	3.2	.1	6.8	.2	1.1	8.1		8.2	11.4
	9.8	1.0	11.5	2.5	1.1	15.1		16.1	25.9

Live saw timber on commercial forest land

[Billions of board feet]

	Private	Government						Total Government	Grand total
		State and local	Federal						
			National forests	Bureau of Land Management	Other	Total Federal			
Western Oregon	131.2	13.1	134.2	58.4	0.4	193.0		206.1	337.3
Eastern Oregon	22.2	.5	62.1	1.5	10.2	73.8		74.3	96.5
	153.4	13.6	196.3	59.9	10.6	266.8		288.4	433.8

Source: "Timber Resources for America's Future," Forest Service, U.S. Department of Agriculture, Forest Reserves Report No. 14.

These private holdings in timber were acquired from the public domain largely in the decade 1900–10. In the 1890's, in anticipation of a move west the lumbermen of the Great Lakes States sent their cruisers (the men who systematically examine forests to estimate quantity and quality of timber) into the forests of the Northwest and California. As the new century began, the rush to acquire timberlands was fully underway.

The lumber baron was one of the figures of the post-Civil War era which Mark Twain called the "gilded age" and Vernon Parrington would bitingly term "The Great Barbecue," although possibly the greatest of them, Frederick Weyerhaeuser, lived without the ostentation and publicity usually associated with the barons. The fortunes amassed by those whose baronies were timber came, for the most part, from an ultimate rise in the value of their timber holdings.

In the first decade of the 20th century, the timber baron, along with other economic barons, was the object of attack, first by the muckrakers, and secondly by the Federal Government, which made a close study of timber holdings to determine the extent of monopoly control of standing timber. Actually, economic law was to flay the timbermen much more effectively than the muckrakers. After 1907, the "lumber barons" needed sympathy.

The 40 years from 1906 to 1946 were difficult ones for the timber industry. The timbered public lands had been sought at a time when a timber famine was freely predicted and money to purchase timberland was easily available on the happy premise that such an investment was a gilt-edged, longtime investment, a type of thought not unknown in the 1950's with respect to the long-term investment merits of other depletable natural resources.

The famine did not eventuate.[6] In fact a chronic depression to which the adversities of the acute depression of 1930's were added laid hold of the timber industry. The consumption of lumber, per capita and absolute, declined steadily from 1906.[7] Under such conditions timberland holders looked in vain for a spectacular rise in timberland values. Stumpage values remained fairly static until 1948,[8] while the holding costs doubled the investment every 10 years.[9] Until 1907 the speculative rise kept ahead of the carrying costs, for in the decade 1900–1910 the rise in timberland values was about 10 percent per year but the rise leveled off beginning about 1910 to a disappointing 2 percent per year.[10]

The timbermen of the Northwest and Oregon who had floated timber bonds to purchase timberland were committed to their amortized repayment.[11] The Northwest did not get to wait for the "sugaring off," the increase in value with depletion of standing timber. The investment had to be realized in manufacture when the speculative rise would no longer carry the holding costs. To meet the repayment on bonds, lumber had to be manufactured and sent to a glutted market even when manufacturing costs were higher than sale value. The timber industry suffered an endemic overproduction until World War II, a production based in large measure on overcapitalized timber holdings. Although Oregon has been the site of the Nation's largest timber resources, it did not become the largest lumber producing State until 1938 when that position passed from Washington, which had held it from 1905.

Oregon's forest industries are its ranking business, accounting for over 80 percent of the manufacturing payroll in employing 90,000 persons. The value of all forest products manufactured is nearly $1 billion annually. This activity is based increasingly on the Government timber but the private holdings have had the predominant part in the past and will undoubtedly continue to have a very important part in the future.

By and large, the private holdings embrace the best and more accessible timber. The greater part of this timberland, as has been mentioned, came into private ownership in the speculative boom of

---

6 "Forest Resources of the Pacific Northwest," pp. 29, 41.

7 Bureau of the Census, "Historical Statistics of the United States, 1789–1945" (Washington, 1949, p. 125). Bureau of the Census, Industry Division, Facts for Industry series, "Lumber and Mill Statistics, 1957."

8 "Historical Statistics of the United States, 1789–1945," p. 125.

9 Ise, "The United States Forest Policy," p. 358.

10 Ibid., pp. 357–358.

11 Ise, "The United States Forest Policy," pp. 357–358.

1900–10. Three U.S. laws and one grant to the State of Oregon governed the disposition of these great forest tracts: The Homestead Act (especially the commutation provision which permitted an occupant to purchase his homestead for $1.25 per acre after a 14 months' residence); the Timber and Stone Act of 1878; the Forest Lieu Act and related acts which made the Northern Pacific land grant the base for large timber holdings in Washington and Oregon; and the indemnity school lands originating in the grant to the State of Oregon.

THE COMMUTED HOMESTEAD

The importance of the commuted homestead in Oregon timberland acquisition is very important although difficult to detail. Its use to acquire timberland was a violation of the spirit and often of the letter of the Homestead Act, justified in western thinking by the feeling that, whatever the law might say, in effect it meant that every man and woman should be entitled to at least 160 acres of public domain. There was no adequate means under the prevailing land disposition laws for lumbermen to acquire timberland in adequate units. Millmen who own their own lumber want to own or reasonably control a 20 year "cut." To acquire such holdings in Oregon, timbermen resorted to subterfuge. The commuted homestead offered it conveniently.

The homestead system anticipated a 160-acre farm as a family freehold. Commuted homesteads were largely taken by professional people in towns [12] and could be sold immediately after proof to either timbermen or timberland brokers. Strictly speaking, a commuted homestead in the timber regions was acquired for timber and not for a home.[13] The Homestead Act was also a means of fraudulently acquiring public land by "dummy entry," that is, by getting individuals to take out a homestead claim, "prove up," and then have the title passed to the instigator with a cash fee paid to the entryman for his trouble. It is, of course, difficult to gage exactly the number of "dummy entries" in acquiring timberland. "Dummy entries" were a western custom, and there were indictments in Oregon for their use in Klamath County in acquiring timberlands.[14]

THE TIMBER AND STONE ACT

The Timber and Stone Act of 1878 was a means of purchasing timber in 160-acre units in California, Oregon, and Nevada and Washington for a minimum of $2.50 per acre [15] which was standard for 30 years. Only one Timber and Stone Act claim was allowed to an individual who had to set forth in an affidavit at the time of application that he did not apply for the claim's purchase on speculation, but in good faith to "appropriate it to his own exclusive use and benefit." [16] Having filed application and published a legal description of the land, a claimant waited 90 days until he paid the purchase price and the patent was issued.

The publication of timber claim notices was a bonanza for the smalltown papers of Oregon. Stephen A. Douglas Puter noted in his

[12] "Senate Documents," 60th Cong., 2d sess., No. 676, pt. 3, p. 391. During this investigation, the chief of special investigators of the General Land Office was H. H. Schwartz, later (1937–43) U.S. Senator from Wyoming.

[13] Ibid., p. 390.

[14] The Oregonian, May 4, 1906.

[15] Stat. L., XX, 89.

[16] Ibid.

"Looters of the Public Domain" (written while he was in jail) that one country editor in Prineville had printed 1,500 timber claim notices in 6 weeks in 1902, receiving $10 per notice, and this on an old press which could not have cost more than $50.[17]

The Timber and Stone Act was the homestead principle applied to the timberland—one small parcel of timberland to a great number of people. It left its mark on the timber ownership pattern in the Northwest. The Timber and Stone Act's popularity as a means of acquiring Oregon timber is clearly set forth in the statistics. From 1878 to 1935, 3,812,303 acres were patented under its terms.[18] Over one-tenth of the land in private ownership in Oregon, or 34 percent of the 11 million acres of privately held timberland, was patented under this act.

The Timber and Stone Act was popular because it was a cash transaction involving no residence or pretense at residence. Although the law required that the claimant swear that he was taking the claim for his own use and benefit, judicial interpretation gave this a wide latitude, the courts ruling that a person could, between first filing and final proof, contract to sell the claim.[19] Actually, the only benefit an individual could get from a 160-acre timber claim was to sell it at one time or another.

The Timber and Stone Act was a convenient way to double a $500 investment in 90 days. The claim, if it were in an area where timber companies or timber brokers were active, could be sold immediately at $5 or $6 per acre,[20] or $800 to $960 per claim. The Weyerhaeuser Timber Co., whose holdings make it singly the most dominant timber company in the Northwest, did not deal directly with the Government in acquiring their timber holdings. A part of them were purchased through the Northern Pacific. Their pine holdings in the Klamath country were acquired by purchasing individual claims at $5 and $6 to block the Oregon and California odd-numbered sections.[21]

TIMBERLAND LOCATORS

A part of the cost of the Timber and Stone Act claims was a locator's fee. In the timber buying boom, professional locators were busy selecting timber, checking the title and offering to locate it for individuals for a fee which ranged from $100 to $250 per claim. Sometimes locators would lend the money with which to purchase a claim. In that case, the purchaser would assign the claim to the locator and receive a nominal sum for his "timber right." Needless to say, locators did a "land office" business in the timber boom. There were "honest brokers" among them. There were also "sharpsters." A receiver at the Roseburg Land Office, in a long letter to the Oregonian in 1900 relating the highlights of the timberland situation that year, noted that the locators then operating were doing a legitimate service but that previously there had been trouble about selling non-

[17] S. A. D. Puter and Horace Stevens, "Looters of the Public Domain" (Portland, 1908), p. 83.

[18] "Senate Documents," 58th Cong., 3d sess., No. 189, pp. 186–187, and a recapitulation furnished by the Bureau of Land Management on Feb. 7, 1951.

[19] *U.S.* v. *Budd*, 144 U.S. 154; and *Williamson* v. *U.S.*, 207 U.S. 425, 460.

[20] "Senate Documents," 60th Cong., 2d sess., No. 676, pt. 3, p. 388.

[21] Sara Jenkins Salo, "Timber Concentration in the Pacific Northwest With Special Reference to the Timber Holdings of the Southern Pacific Railroad, the Northern Pacific Railroad and the Weyerhaeuser Timber Company" (Ann Arbor, 1945), p. 15.

timbered claims for $400.[22] In this same letter, J. Henry Booth, the receiver, noted that some Oregonians at last were selecting timberland but the largest selections were still going to easterners represented by locators from Michigan, Wisconsin, and Minnesota. Another type of company operating in that year was one which had sent its crusiers to Oregon to buy small claims for resale when a good block was established.

The activities of one company of locators can be partially reconstructed from their correspondence now in the Oregon Collection of the University of Oregon Library. These locators advertised far and wide. William Hawks and George S. Canfield charged $100 to $150 for locating Timber and Stone Act claims and homesteads and $1.25 per acre for furnishing school indemnity "base," [23] which made the cost of the State land $2.50 to the purchaser. A letter which clearly reveals a prevailing motive in acquiring a Timber and Stone Act claim was an answer to a Hawk-Canfield advertisement:

> My wife and self desire to get a claim each, provided we can dispose of the same directly after proving up on them. I also know at least six men here who can be depended upon to do the right thing by anyone who can place them on claims, and guarantee a profitable sale when they prove up.[24]

Canfield and Hawks built a network of agents centering in Portland. They solicited agents in the East offering to pay them $25 out of every location fee from persons directed to them by the eastern representatives. They also divided the location fee with local men who cruised the claims, checked the titles, escorted people to view them, and guided buyers through the formalities of the land office.[25] Stephen A. D. Puter in his confession of land-grabbing has described taking a party of 108 persons to view tracts of ponderosa pine in Crook County. Entire families, numbering from 2 to 15 persons, were in the party. In this instance, the deal was not completed because of the death of the midwestern lumberman who was contracted to buy up the claims.

Puter has described the locating activity in Crook County in the summer of 1902 when the roads from Shaniko (the end of the railroad) and Bend and Prineville were lined with travelers coming and going into the timber. Puter took one group of 45 to view a ponderosa tract.

> The concourse of vehicles resembled a Sunday turnout in Golden Gate Park * * * only of course the equipages were not quite so swell.[26]

"They were honest in their own way" is a qualified judgment upon timber locators. When dealing with them, according to one who has, it was essential to know the section corners.[27] The prospective purchaser of a Timber and Stone Act claim who was viewing a tract with a locator had to know that the tract he was viewing was the same as the one for which a legal description was furnished, else he might find

[22] The Oregonian, Aug. 12, 1900. There is a striking similarity between the activities of timberland brokers then and oil and gas lease brokers now. In the timberland there were those who acted responsibly as brokers in assembling blocks of timberland of sufficient size to make them marketable. They have their counterparts in oil and gas lease brokers working under the Mineral Leasing Act of 1920 who assemble blocks of suitable size for drilling. There were also timberland brokers trafficking in the instruments of timberland ownership and willing to sell to any buyer regardless. They too have their counterparts in the oil and gas leasing play.

[23] William Hawks and George S. Canfield to Adelia M. Casey, Dec. 10, 1902. Business correspondence of William Hawks and George S. Canfield, November 1902–January 1903. Oregon Collection, University of Oregon Library.

[24] J. L. Boyle to William Hawks, Oct. 15, 1902. Ibid.

[25] William Hawks and George S. Canfield to Hunter Land Co., Dec. 10, 1902; to W. A. Leonard, Jan. 26, 1903. Ibid.

[26] Puter, "Looters of the Public Domain," pp. 81–83.

[27] E. M. Bubb, interview, Feb. 21, 1951.

ultimately that he had actually purchased a tract of jack pine or juniper.

Final Timber and Stone Act acreage

1880–89	139, 527	1910–19	192, 772
1890–99	346, 717	1920–29	56, 417
1900–1909	3, 077, 535	1930–35	2, 003

Source: Computed from "Senate Documents," 58th Cong., 3d sess., No. 189, pp. 186–187, and a recapitulation furnished by the Bureau of Land Management, Feb. 7, 1951.

Locators and timbermen who were buying Timber and Stone Act claims organized big parties to take to the timbers and then to the land office to file the claims. A Government investigator asserted that one big Oregon holding was acquired by bringing out a trainload of schoolteachers from Minnesota one summer and having them all file Timber and Stone Act claims.[28]

The greatest acreage of land acquired under the Timber and Stone Act was, naturally enough, in the timber-buying boom of 1900–1910. In the years 1900 through 1909, 3,077,536 acres were purchased as Timber and Stone Act claims. The highest single year was 1903 when 645,578 acres were purchased. In the same year, Washington, second-ranking State that year in Timber and Stone Act acreage, had claims amounting to 287,578 acres. The end of the timberland buying boom can be read in the Timber and Stone yearly totals. In 1909, 281,899 acres were purchased in Oregon. In 1910, that total fell precipitately to 34,209 acres. The sharp drop in yearly totals between 1904, when 489,734, and 1905, when 191,284 acres were purchased, is accounted for by a series of land fraud indictments and convictions in Oregon (the most outstanding being the conviction of U.S. Senator John H. Mitchell).[29]

The Timber and Stone Act and the Homestead Act imparted a pattern of scattered ownership of Oregon timber, a fact often overlooked by the attention given to large holdings. Even John Ise in his careful monograph "U.S. Forest Policy" asserts that—

> not over a fractional part of 1 percent of the timber purchased under this act [the Timber and Stone Act] is now held by the men and women who made the entries.[30]

Ise was basing his statement on material in the U.S. Bureau of Corporations, "The Lumber Industry," which he himself correctly declared was—

> written with the too-evident purpose of proving the existence of something approaching a monopoly condition in the timber and lumber industry * * *.[31]

Although many Timber and Stone Act claims passed from the hands of original owners, many must have been held, either because they could not be sold or in anticipation of higher stumpage value. The most recent timber resources appraisal shows 23,914 owners in Oregon holding 867,000 acres of timberland in average units of 36 acres, ranging to 100 acres.[32] These holdings undoubtedly represent timberland held incidental to other activity, i.e., farming or grazing; and the land upon the timber stands was acquired from the public domain most probably for reasons removed from its value as timberland.

[28] "Senate Documents," 60th Cong., 2d sess., No. 676, pt. 3, p. 389.
[29] The Oregonian, Nov. 26, 1904. See ch. IX.
[30] Ise, "U.S. Forest Policy," p. 226.
[31] Ibid., p. 316.
[32] "Timber Resources."

Ninety-one percent of the timberland is held in units above 100 acres and the greatest proportion of this land was probably acquired for its timber.

Twenty percent of Oregon's timber acreage is held by some 10,278 owners in blocs ranging from 100 to 500 acres for an average holding of 197 acres.[33] This, after all the blocking which has taken place over the years, suggests that the amount of timberland transferred, covertly or otherwise, from small to large holding has been overestimated. The holdings in this class, it is reasonable to anticipate, originated in the Timber and Stone Act claims and by the operation of the homestead law. These acts secured the diversity of ownership which was the homestead ideal.

Timberland ownership in Oregon

[By size of holdings]

	Acres	Percent	Number of owners	Percent	Average size
0 to 100 acres	867,000	9	23,914	66	36
100 to 500 acres	2,010,000	20	10,278	28	197
500 to 5,000 acres	2,144,000	22	1,917	5	1,120
5,000 to 50,000 acres	2,129,000	22	127		16,800
Over 50,000 acres	2,618,000	27	15		174,000

Source: "Timber Resources for America's Future."

At the same time the adroit manipulation of other public laws made it possible to assemble large blocks of timberland for a concentration of ownership in juxtaposition to the diversity imparted by the Timber and Stone Act and the Homestead Act. This acquisition is demonstrated in the latest timber resources appraisal which shows, for example, that 27 percent of the timberland of Oregon is held by 15 operators holding in blocks in excess of 50,000 acres with an average holding of 174,000 acres. Another 22 percent of Oregon timberland is held by 127 operators in units ranging from 5,000 to 50,000 acres for an average of 16,800 acres.

The large blocs embrace the best, most accessible timber. The smaller holdings embraced the less desirable and less accessible timberland, although the change from logging by railroad to logging by truck and other mechanical innovations has nullified some of the disadvantages which existed when the first cruises were made at the turn of the century.

THE NORTHERN PACIFIC GRANT AND THE FOREST LIEU ACT

These large holdings had their origin in the Northern Pacific land grant, the Oregon & California land grant, two wagon road grants, and the school indemnity lands of Oregon. Although only a small part of the original Northern Pacific grant was in Oregon, by 1914 264,520 acres of Oregon timberland had passed to private ownership through the Northern Pacific grant.[34]

When the national forests were created, beginning in 1891, Washington was strewn with the odd-numbered sections of the Northern Pacific land grant which had been 25,600 acres per mile (the Northern Pacific grant was double the standard in the territories and Washing-

[33] Ibid.

[34] Bureau of Corporations, "The Lumber Industry," II, 77.

ton was a territory at time of construction). In the Civil Appropriations Act of 1898, the Northern Pacific was empowered to take any odd-numbered section, not valuable for mineral or stone, in any State or territory in which its grant existed when the Northern Pacific would relinquish to the United States its rights in any unsurveyed sections within its original grant upon which there was a valid claimant.[35] When the Mount Rainier National Park was established in 1899, the act authorized the Northern Pacific to relinquish its sections within the park and in the Pacific forest reserve and to receive in lieu any nonmineral public lands in any State through which the Northern Pacific passed.[36]

These acts were known in timber circles as the "scripper" acts because the Northern Pacific sold its rights to these lieu lands by scrip which became a favorite medium for buying timber. Timberlands could be purchased in unlimited quantity and in large blocks. As scrip became available syndicates became active in its use to buy Oregon timberlands. One letter writer to the Oregonian asserted, in 1906, that there was no timber by 1901 which was not familiar to the scripping syndicate cruisers.[37] The writer further asserted that the Timber and Stone Act claims were located on the lands passed over by the "scrippers." J. Henry Booth, receiver of the land office at Roseburg, reported in a long account to the Oregonian in 1900 that the busy days at the Roseburg land office were caused by the placing of Northern Pacific scrip. At the same time, scrip from the Cascade reserve and the Oregon school indemnity lands was eagerly sought by timber men to block together tracts with an eye to good logging conditions.[38]

Frederick Weyerhaeuser, who late in life said, "the only time I have lost money was when I didn't buy," purchased 900,000 acres in one sale from the Northern Pacific at $6 per acre.[39] Forty-six percent of the Weyerhaeuser holdings in Oregon, according to a 1914 study, originated in the Northern Pacific grant.[40] It held at that time 380,599 acres.

The Weyerhaeuser holdings in western Oregon were acquired through the Northern Pacific, while its pine holdings in Jackson and Klamath Counties were acquired by purchasing holdings already blocked by other companies and by a 13,223-acre holding acquired by a subsidiary from the Oregon and California grant.[41] The lands acquired by Northern Pacific scrip were fine timberlands although the original base lands were not as valuable, many of the sections in the Mount Rainier National Park being rocky and untimbered.

By 1914, 264,520 acres of Oregon timberland had passed to private ownership through the Northern Pacific grant. Weyerhaeuser, by all odds, was the biggest purchaser with 177,461 acres. Next in rank was C. A. Smith with 12,170.[42]

Besides the special lieu acts for the Northern Pacific, there was a general Forest Lieu Act. Although called such, it was really a section within the Sundry Civil Appropriations Act of 1897, which provided that any tract within a public forest covered by a bona fide unper-

35 Stat. L., XXX, 620.
36 Stat. L., XXX, 994.
37 The Oregonian, Feb. 10, 1906.
38 The Oregonian, Aug. 12, 1900.
39 Bureau of Corporations, "The Lumber Industry," I, 237.
40 Bureau of Corporations, "The Lumber Industry," II, 55.
41 Ibid., I, 55–56.
42 Ibid., II, 77.

fected claim might be relinquished by a settler or owner who might select in lieu any tract of the same size on any land open to settlement.[43]

The State of Oregon as owner of all sections numbered 16 and 36 within the national forests would have been a major beneficiary of the Forest Lieu Act. However, Oregon was selling its public lands rather than holding them. The Forest Lieu Act made then even more desirable as timberland. For one thing, land could be bought from the State for $1.25 per acre; it was an inexpensive means of acquiring "base" upon which to make lieu selections in blocks outside the national forests.

The Forest Lieu Act stimulated a special type of land fraud which sought to create even more extensive forest reserves than were necessary with a scheme to have inside information on boundary locations so that school sections could be quickly purchased to be used as base for clocking units outside the national forests.[44]

The Forest Lieu Act and the school indemnity lands were a favorite means of acquiring timberland because they permitted convenient consolidation of holdings. The purchase of timber is not a mere purchase of trees, but a purchase with consideration of the factors which determine logging. The value of timberland per acre rises with its inclusion in larger blocks of timberland. The logging chance is greater on large blocks and the protection costs are less.

The convenience of locating large blocks of timber with forest scrip is seen in one operation described by Stephen Puter, mentioned several times previously for his connections with Oregon land scandals. Puter was a timberland locator who could be both honest and dishonest in getting together blocks of timber. He was the intermediary between timber men and individuals exercising their homestead or timber rights. In this instance, Puter was operating strictly within the law. On advice of his attorney, Franklin Pierce Mays, who was, as Puter noted, an expert at operating "close hauled" to the law, Puter was using the Timber and Stone Act to attempt to block a unit of ponderosa pine in Crook County. He had 108 persons ready to file Timber and Stone Act claims when his backer in the Midwest died. His claimants withdrew from the arrangements when they would not follow the complicated maneuvers Puter proposed to offset the death of the backer.[45]

When these arrangements failed, Puter found a timberman in Portland with forest scrip. Puter offered to acquire the 108 claims for the timberman by filing his scrip on them for a fee of 50 cents an acre. The man accepted and obtained title at one stroke to 17,280 acres. The Government lost the $43,000 which it would have received had the land been taken under the Timber and Stone Act.[46]

THE SOUTHERN PACIFIC AS TIMBER OWNER

Before it lost the Oregon & California grant in 1916, the Southern Pacific was the greatest timberland owner in the Nation. The Oregon & California grant carried 71 billion feet of timber, by a 1913 estimate, of the 105 billion owned by the Southern Pacific.[47] When it halted sales of the Oregon & California lands in 1903, the Southern Pacific

[43] Stat. L., XXX, 36.
[44] Land fraud will be treated in ch. IX.
[45] Puter, "Looters of the Public Domain," p. 90.
[46] Puter, "Looters of the Public Domain," p. 90.
[47] Bureau of Corporations, "The Lumber Industry," I, 15–16

still retained 72 percent of the original grant.[48] Thirteen percent had been sold in large units to timber interests. The Southern Pacific sold 369,469 acres of timberland from the Oregon & California grant. The single most important purchaser was the Booth-Kelly Lumber Co. which acquired 68,629 acres.[49] The Oregon & California lands were in alternate sections, and their ownership left holders with the necessity of acquiring adjoining sections.

Besides the railroad grants there were two wagon road grants in Oregon which also furnished a means of acquiring timberland, again in alternate sections. The Oregon Central Military Wagon Road grant, which extended from Eugene, at the head of the Willamette Valley, to the eastern boundary via the Willamette Pass, the Klamath Indian Reservation and Lakeview, was heavily timbered with Douglas-fir on the western slope of the Cascades. It also passed near the ponderosa stands of Klamath and Lake counties. The land grant was sold by the construction company and was owned in the 1900's by the California & Oregon Land Co. which was a Booth-Kelly subsidiary. This gave Booth-Kelly control of the timber on the western portion of the grant.

The Oregon Central grant was also the means of blocking 87,000 acres of ponderosa pine on the Klamath Indian Reservation. The old military road passed through the reservation and it had acquired 110,000 acres in alternate sections through the reservation. This interfered with the orderly allotment of tribal lands to individual Indians. As has been previously related, the Federal Government attempted to nullify the patents to reservation land and failing that, traded 87,000 acres in a compact block of ponderosa pine for the 110 acres of alternate sections.

The Booth-Kelly holdings illustrated the diverse means of acquiring timber land. Their holdings were acquired through the purchase of the Oregon and California lands and the ownership of the Oregon Central Military Wagon Road grant. These holdings were supplemented and blocked up by 90,000 acres presumably acquired from individual entrymen who had taken them under the Timber and Stone Act and the Homestead Act.[50]

The Willamette Valley and Cascade Mountain Wagon Road grant from Albany to the Idaho border had 178,720 acres of heavy timber on the western portion, which in 1913 belonged to the Oregon & Western Colonization Co. The company was selling the non-timbered portion in eastern Oregon but retaining the timbered lands. The Coos Bay Wagon Road grant of 100,000 acres was also owned in 1913 by timber interests, but the grant was reconveyed to the United States in 1919 for violation of the sale limitations of the granting act.

In 1914, the Bureau of Corporations listed 68 timber owners holding 4,272,331 acres with 236.2 billion feet.[51] The greatest of these was the Southern Pacific with 1,907,236 acres bearing 70.5 billion feet.

[48] Ibid., II, 75–76.

[49] Ibid.

[50] Bureau of Corporations, "The Lumber Industry," II, p. 58.

[51] Ibid., II, p. 66. This monograph was written with the too evident purpose of finding tendencies toward monopoly. It did not discuss the problems of holding timber, nor did it emphasize that legal proceedings had been taken to restore the Oregon and California grant. It overlooked altogether the amount of timber-land in small ownership, predicting that it would be under the complete control of the big holdings. While its statistics are very helpful in viewing the Oregon timberlands in 1913, its assumptions, especially those covering gaps in evidence, must be carefully read.

Weyerhaeuser was second with 250,430 acres carrying 15.9 billion feet. Railroad and wagon road grants and the school indemnity lands fostered this concentration. The Timber and Stone Act and the Homestead Act imparted a great diffusion of ownership, particularly in the more inaccessible reaches of the timber country.

A complete monopoly of standing timber did not materialize. Between 1910 and 1920 a distinct change worked out in ownership. The timber famine which encouraged premature investment in Oregon timber failed to make its heralded appearance and the price of standing timber was stabilized. The fixed charges of carrying timberland now became a burden. On one hand this promoted a concentration as the cheapness of standing timber prompted strong investors who could meet the carrying costs to buy up small inaccessible units.[52] On the other hand, the carrying costs forced some who were holding for the speculative increases, which leveled off after 1910, to sell their holdings or portions of them.[53] In 1916, the United States recovered the Oregon and California grant and one-sixth of Oregon's timber was returned to public ownership. In 1920, 17,000 timber holdings in Oregon were less than 1 billion feet.[54] An Oregon lumberman in 1923 asserted that there were 30,000 timber owners in Oregon and only 699 logging concerns.[55]

PRESENT OWNERSHIP PATTERN

Today there are 36,000 private owners of timberland but only 1,200 manufacturing plants. One-half of this private timber is owned, as previously discussed, by 142 operators whose holdings however are outdistanced by various units of government mainly the Federal, which owns 60 percent of the timber.

Public land laws have promoted, therefore, both a diversity of owners and concentration of owners. Public policy has not yet come to grips with the means of assuring the highest productivity on these forest lands, either private or public. On the smaller private holdings periodic cuttings followed by silviculture practices give promise of permanent productivity. On the larger holdings the procedure is an annual one. With respect to the public timberland, upon which a large number of operators depend for stumpage, the prime need is for access roads which will permit cutting which will promote the continual growth of the forests. In the past private timber has been heavily cut while public timber has been cut at less than its sustained yield capability.

For all practical purposes the disposition of the timberlands has been completed. In the future the problems of the timberlands will be those of management, private and public, but of course the base upon which that management must rest has been laid down by the land disposition laws which governed the transfer from public to private ownership.

---

52 U.S. Forest Service, "Timber Depletion, Lumber Prices, Lumber Exports and Concentration of Timber Ownership" (Washington, 1920), p. 61.

53 Ibid.

54 Ibid.

55 Robert W. Vinnedge, "The Pacific Northwest Lumber Industry and Its Development, Yale University Lumber Industry Series No. 4" (New Haven, 1923), p. 19.

In any event a new era has dawned in the timber industry which moved from the Penobscot and the Kennebec to the Columbia on the operating premise of "cut and move." "We'd still be logging in Wisconsin," as one oldtime Oregon logger once said, "except for the logs we took out in the dark."

The day of "cut and move" has set. The time of "cut and grow some more" has dawned. The growth will take place on both the public timberlands and the private timberlands to the extent that trained minds are mobilized to meet the challenge of fostering more timber for the needs of a people whose principal commitment in the foreseeable future will be the test to prove that a democratically free society is still the best hope of mankind.

CHAPTER IX

LAND FRAUD IN THE TIMBER

A generation of easy, fraudulent expropriation of the public lands was climaxed in Oregon on July 3, 1905, when John Mitchell, who had served Oregon in the U.S. Senate 22 years and had risen to the chairmanship of the Interoceanic Canal Committee, was convicted of receiving fees for expediting claims before the General Land Office. Mitchell, leader of the Mitchell faction of the Republican Party in Oregon, 70 years old, with a long chest-length beard, a patriarch of the Senate, had entered Oregon politics almost immediately on his arrival in 1860, having left his native Pennsylvania and a wife behind him that same year. His political fortunes waxed and waned in Oregon for 45 years so that his terms in the Senate were not consecutive. He was elected in 1872, again in 1884 and 1890. He lost in 1896 because his stand on the money issue pleased neither gold nor silver men. He was elected for his last term in 1900.[1]

He was "the most popular leader of his generation in Oregon," of impressive physical appearance and had power as a speaker as well as being adept at the "politician's art." [2] The Oregonian, whose editor, Harvey Scott, had contested Mitchell's power in the Republican Party, printed a long sketch of Mitchell's life at the time of his indictment. It dwelt upon changing his name from John Hipple to John Hipple Mitchell, his desertion of his wife and other details of domestic infidelity, but concluded that he did have power over men. Mitchell had no eloquence, but he did have persuasiveness and—

> * * * a faculty of political perception and organization; an art of winning admirers by a handshake or a glance * * * in spite of his impaired ability to remember names and faces as he once used to do.[3]

The Mitchell case is admirably suited to recital by a historian. It is typical in illustrating the manner in which land fraud rings operated. It is unique and even sensational in having as its main character a U.S. Senator.

The events which led to Mitchell's conviction in 1905 began in December 1902 when Binger Hermann was dismissed as Commissioner of the General Land Office by Ethan Allen Hitchcock, Secretary of the Interior. Hermann, an Oregonian, had served 12 years in Congress, and before that as an official of the district land office in Roseburg.

Binger Hermann was dismissed as Commissioner of the General Land Office for his failure to pass the first report on the Benson-Hyde conspiracy to the Secretary of the Interior. While William J. Burns, ace Treasury detective, was uncovering the Benson-Hyde fraud in California and Washington, D.C., other investigations were going for-

[1] "The Dictionary of American Biography," XIII, pp. 53–54.
[2] Ibid.
[3] The Oregonian, Feb. 12, 1905.

56227—60——7

ward in Oregon. The Secretary of the Interior seemingly was eager to prosecute Oregon fraud cases to vindicate his dismissal of Hermann.[4]

Such dismissal for "loose methods" was no debarment to public favor in Oregon, for Hermann was elected almost immediately to take the place of a Representative who had died in office. Some assert that his election was secured when he managed to get himself photographed with Theodore Roosevelt on the observation platform of the Roosevelt train during a Portland visit.[5] Not only did Hermann go back to Congress, where he had served before his appointment to the General Land Office, but he was assigned to the Public Lands Committee. A close friend of Mitchell's asserted that the Oregon trials were all "framed" by Theodore Roosevelt because Mitchell, as chairman of the Senate Interoceanic Canal Committee, was opposed to Roosevelt's procedures.[6]

STEPHEN A. DOUGLAS PUTER AND "11–7" CASE

The Government investigations into the dealings of Stephen A. Douglas Puter, who styled himself "king of the Oregon land fraud ring," led to the implication of Mitchell and his ultimate conviction. "Steve" Puter, whose title rests upon a conviction and the book he wrote in the leisure of a 17-month sojourn in the Multnomah County jail, was an intermediary between timbermen and those who took out individual 160-acre claims. Puter was a promoter who usually sought a backer who would promise to take a tract of timberland from Puter when he had it all blocked together.

One such deal which ended in Puter's conviction and Mitchell's implication was known as the 11–7 case for its involved fraudulent entries instituted by Puter and his colleagues during 1900 in township 11 south, range 7 east of the Willamette meridian. The township was deliberately chosen as being remote and inaccessible, high in the Cascade Range near Mount Jefferson. Its real value to Puter or to the person who took it off Puter's hands was as "base" for "lieu" selections as the township was within the Cascade Forest Reserve.

The conspiracy to defraud consisted of Puter's prevailing on 10 persons to enter 12 homestead claims (2 people signed for additional claims by using fictitious names) in township 11–7 and to assert that they were living on the claims at the time the Cascade Forest Reserve was created. None of the 10 had ever seen the land, according to Puter, and no one lived within 30 miles of the township.[7]

Puter and an accomplice, Horace Greeley McKinley, paid sums ranging from $150 to $800 to these "claimants," and deeds were made to Mrs. Emma Watson, who had also taken one of the claims as Emma Porter.[8] In all, Puter and his principal partner, Horace Greeley McKinley, paid $3,800 for the claims.[9] They arranged to have the final proofs filed before the deputy county clerk of Linn County, Robert B. Montague, to whom Puter claims to have paid $100 per claim for accepting final filings.[10] The lawyer who handled

---

4 The Oregonian, Dec. 11, 1904; Lincoln Steffens, "The Taming of the West," American Magazine LXIV (1907), p. 505.
5 Ibid. The picture is reproduced in Puter, "Looters of the Public Domain," p. 386.
6 William H. Galvani, "Recollections of J. F. Stevens and Senator Mitchell," O.H.Q., XLIV (1943) 320–321.
7 Puter, "Looters of the Public Domain," p. 50.
8 Ibid.
9 Ibid.
10 Ibid., p. 48.

the legal papers and acted as general contact man with the district land office was Daniel Webster Tarpeley, known in the "looters" circles as "Lookout Dan."

The final papers were filed in October 1900. For reasons not known to Puter, the claims came under investigation. He was warned of the first investigation by "Lookout Dan" Tarpeley, who told him that C. E. Loomis, special agent for the Oregon City District Land Office, had been ordered to investigate the claims in 11–7. Puter claimed that he paid Loomis $500 to investigate the claims out of order and promised him another $500 when the claims were patented.[11] He also arranged with J. A. W. Heidicke, of Detroit, Oreg., to show Loomis claims in another township. Heidicke was, seemingly, exerting gentle blackmail on Puter as he well knew that there were no homesteaders in that township. Besides $350, he wanted Puter to use his influence with Binger Hermann, then Commissioner of the General Land Office, to get an appointment for Heidicke as a forest ranger.[12]

Loomis rendered a favorable report, complete with affidavits from 6 of the 12 "homesteaders" and including affidavits from citizens of Detroit. Another investigation was ordered, however. This time, Puter claims he placed $500 in escrow for Salmon B. Ormsby, superintendent of the Cascade Forest Reserve, who was ordered to investigate the nature of the improvements in 11–7.[13] Ormsby made his investigation in January 1902, but Puter could not be certain of its contents.

This uncertainty brought Senator Mitchell and Commissioner Hermann into dealings. On advice of his attorney, Franklin Pierce Mays, Puter went to Washington in February 1902 with a letter from Mays to Senator Mitchell. Mrs. Emma Watson arrived there shortly after because Mays had advised that the Senator might put himself out to do a favor for a lady.[14]

Puter called on Mitchell and Hermann and found that all the reports on the 12 claims were in the General Land Office, but that it would be several months before they would be acted upon. Mitchell then wrote an affidavit setting forth that Mrs. Watson would lose her investment in the 12 claims. She had been represented as a widow who had borrowed money to purchase claims. Mrs. Watson signed the affidavit prepared by Mitchell, and Hermann made the claims a special order of business. He reported to Puter that they could not be patented and suggested that Puter return to Oregon and get more affidavits from the 12 original entrymen.[15] This Puter was reluctant to do. He went to Mitchell, who advised substantially the same thing. Here, then, Puter asserted, he took out two $1,000 bills and gave them to Mitchell.

Mitchell at first refused them, according to Puter. "Mr. Puter, I cannot think of allowing you to pay that sum of money to me," and he pushed one of the bills back.[16] He promised to see Hermann, and the patents were soon issued. Puter returned to Oregon and sold the 12 claims to Frederick Kribs for $5.25 per acre, totaling $10,080.

---

[11] Ibid., pp. 52–53.
[12] Ibid., pp. 53–54.
[13] Ibid., pp. 57–58.
[14] Ibid., p. 58.
[15] Ibid., p. 61.
[16] Ibid., p. 63.

When Puter reported the negotiations to his attorney, Mays, the attorney, was irritated because Puter paid $1,000:

> Yes, sir; you have ruined the game, Puter, and from this time on, it will be a case of "money talks" or no business, whereas * * * we would get most anything asked for at comparatively little expense.[17]

Puter, Horace McKinley, and Marie Ware were indicted October 27, 1903, for conspiracy to defraud the Government of its public lands. A lengthier indictment was issued March 17, 1904, adding Maud Witt, Frank Walgamot, Harry C. Bauer, and Dan Tarpeley.[18]

After the 11–7 finesse was well underway, Puter and McKinley decided to work the same operation in T. 24 S., R. 1 E., of the Willamette meridian, another remote township high in the Cascades at the headwaters of the Middle Fork of the Willamette River. This time, however, they decided to eliminate the expense of paying people to pose as homesteaders. They decided to use fictitious people and have the papers filed before Marie Ware, the U.S. Commissioner at Eugene, and McKinley's sweetheart.[19] Puter's lawyer, Franklin P. Mays, a one-time U.S. attorney, was also a partner in the 24–1 fraud and was indicted with Puter, Emma Watson, McKinley, and Dan Tarpeley December 24, 1904.[20]

FRANCIS J. HENEY AS SPECIAL PROSECUTOR

The Puter cases were ready for trial when Francis J. Heney was appointed, in October 1903, a special assistant to the Attorney General of the United States to prosecute the Oregon frauds. Heney was an Irishman born "south of Market" in San Francisco. Before his Oregon appointment he had a checkered career, which included expulsion from the University of California for dueling, teaching school in an Idaho mining town, storekeeping and ranching in Arizona, where he went to practice law after getting a degree in San Francisco. He entered the rough and tumble Arizona territorial politics. He killed an Arizona doctor and political boss when the man threatened to shoot him for obtaining a divorce for the doctor's wife.[21]

Oregonians did not like the appointment of this outsider as a special prosecutor. The Portland Bar Association protested his appointment, as did Senator Mitchell, not yet implicated, and Senator Charles W. Fulton; but President Roosevelt and Attorney General Knox both refused to reconsider. Later, Mitchell was to charge Heney with being a California Democrat trying to destroy the reputation of Republicans from Oregon.[22]

Puter asserted that Heney's appointment foiled the scheme of his attorney, Franklin Mays, to have the trials continually postponed and then the indictments dropped, through influence with John H. Hall, the U.S. district attorney for Oregon. Hall attempted to relegate Heney to a minor position in the prosecution. Heney charged this to professional jealousy, but William J. Burns, who had ferreted out the Benson-Hyde system, was working on the Oregon cases and guessed that Hall was shielding people and had purposely chosen to

---

17 Ibid., p. 66.
18 Secretary of the Interior, Report, 1904, p. 22.
19 Puter, "Looters of the Public Domain," p. 68–74.
20 Ibid., p. 442. There is a convenient summary of indictments and cases in Oregon land fraud trials, pp. 442–454.
21 A flamboyant account of Heney's life is given by Lincoln Steffens, "The Making of a Fighter," American Magazine, LXIV (1907), 339–360.
22 Puter, "Looters of the Public Domain," p. 180.

prosecute Puter and his colleagues on the weaker case,[23] the 24–1 case which was inherently weaker because the fictitious entrymen could not, of course, be found to have their allegations proved false.

Heney presented a new indictment against Puter, McKinley, and Tarpeley in March 1904, and they were convicted on December 6, 1904, of conspiracy to defraud the Government of lands in township 11–7.[24] Three days previously, Dr. Frank H. Walgomot had pleaded guilty to signing an affidavit attesting to his residence on one of the homesteads in 11–7.

Lincoln Steffens has written that Heney used Puter to implicate Senator Mitchell.[25] Puter says that he turned on Mitchell for the castigations made against Puter in the press by Mitchell after Puter's conviction.[26] Puter was also angered because his colleagues, Mays and Kribs, would not put up bail for him while he was waiting for a new trial. A newspaper editorial also recorded the rumor that Puter turned against Mitchell because he was promised a fine in place of a jail sentence.[27] Whatever promises had or had not been made, Puter was fined $7,500 and sentenced to 2 years in jail, but pardoned after 17 months in the Multnomah County jail by President Roosevelt in 1907.[28]

TRIAL OF SENATOR MITCHELL

On Puter's testimony before the grand jury that he had given Senator Mitchell money to speed the final patenting in the 11–7 claims, Heney obtained an indictment against Senator Mitchell, January 1, 1905.[29] Just before the Mitchell indictment, Heney requested and received the dismissal of John H. Hall as U.S. Attorney for Oregon. Heney was appointed in his place.[30]

Mitchell hurried back from Washington to appear before the grand jury which indicted him. In a public statement before his indictment, he said:

> I have lived in this State over 44 years. I have served in the U.S. Senate nearly 22 years, and I defy any man to charge me successfully with conduct that is otherwise than honorable, and I am sure I cannot be connected in any manner with any land frauds except by the grossest perjury of self-confessed and convicted thieves and perjurers.[31]

After his indictment, Mitchell returned to Washington and broke Senate precedent by appearing on the floor to answer the indictment. He was warmly received by his colleagues in the Senate.[32] He categorically denied all the charges [33] and recited in great detail his actual dealings with Puter in the 11–7 case. The recital is essentially that given by Puter in "Looters of the Public Domain," except, of course, Mitchell denied the incriminating assertion that he received any money from Puter.

In his Senate explanation, Mitchell said that in the preceding 3 years he had looked into the status of hundreds of land claims for his Oregon constituents without compensation, and added, "I shall

[23] Lincoln Steffens, loc. cit., p. 594.
[24] Secretary of the Interior, report, 1906, p. 27.
[25] Lincoln Steffens, loc. cit., p. 595.
[26] Puter, "Looters of the Public Domain," p. 174.
[27] The Oregonian, Dec. 19, 1904.
[28] Puter, "Looters of the Public Domain," p. 7.
[29] The Oregonian, Jan. 1, 1905.
[30] Ibid.
[31] Ibid., Dec. 31, 1905.
[32] The Oregonian, Jan. 18, 1905.
[33] The speech is reported in the Congressional Record, 58th Cong., 3d sess., pp. 959–963.

continue to do these things for my constituents, so help me God, even at the risk of 100 indictments."[34] Mitchell admitted that he could have been imposed upon by those pressing fraudulent claims. He charged that Puter was implicating him upon a promise of leniency.

Before Mitchell came to trial in June 1905, there were sensational ramifications. Heney obtained the indictment of John H. Hall, the ex-U.S. attorney, for obstructing justice by a plot to discredit Heney with perjured testimony alleging illicit relations between Heney and Marie Ware, the former U.S. commissioner, who had been indicted with Puter but whose indictment, upon Heney's motion, had been dropped. She had been approached by Hall to swear to these illicit relations, but she would not, and she carried the report of the plot to Heney, who obtained Hall's indictment in February 1905.[35] Heney also recommended the removal of U.S. Marshal W. F. Mathews, whom Heney found uncooperative and overfriendly to the defendants.[36]

The original indictment charging Mitchell with receiving $1,000 from Puter was replaced with an indictment on February 1 charging violation of the Federal code which prohibited Senators and other officials from receiving fees for furthering matters in any Government work.[37] The charge against Mitchell involving Puter's alleged payment was congenitally weak. It was the word of a U.S. Senator opposed to that of a convicted "land grabber." Puter in "Looters of the Public Domain" says that he thought a long time of a way to implicate Mitchell with evidence which would stand in court. He finally thought of Frederick A. Kribs, a timber land broker, who represented C. A. Smith, a Minneapolis timberman. Kribs had had dealings with Mitchell, and Puter knew, so he said, that Kribs always paid by check.[38]

The indictment upon which Mitchell was convicted charged that Mitchell had received a fee of $1,750 at a rate of $25 per claim for expediting 70 claims for Frederick A. Kribs.[39] In the matter of fees, Puter records an argument with some of his partners about senatorial fees. Puter was explaining that Mitchell received $25 per claim when one of his partners objected to this payment, saying the other Senator, Charles W. Fulton, was charging only $10.[40] Fulton was never indicted, but he was defeated in the 1908 Republican primaries.[41]

The fees had been paid to the Senator's law firm, Mitchell & Tanner. This brought the partner, Judge Albert H. Tanner, into the case. The two men had had a partnership agreement drawn up in 1901, which made no mention of Land Office fees. Tanner was indicted and pleaded guilty to perjury in shielding Mitchell.[42] Mitchell tried to evade the charge by substituting a predated agreement written in 1905 for the 1901 agreement. In the "new" agreement, it was specially stated that any fees accruing to the firm for General Land Office business would belong exclusively to Tanner. Judge Tanner confessed to perjury to protect his son, Albert H. Tanner, Jr.,

---

[34] Ibid., p. 962.
[35] The Oregonian, Feb. 3, 1905; Feb. 14, 1905. Heney was later shot in court during his prosecutions of municipal corruption in San Francisco; see Robert Glass Cleland, "California in Our Time, 1900–1940" (New York, 1947), p. 22.
[36] The Oregonian, Mar. 14, 1905.
[37] Ibid.
[38] Puter, "Looters of the Public Domain," pp. 185, 208.
[39] The Oregonian, Feb. 2, 1905.
[40] Puter, "Looters of the Public Domain," pp. 88–89.
[41] Scott, "History of the Oregon Country," I, 347.
[42] The Oregonian, Feb. 9, 1905.

who, as his father's stenographer, had written the "new" agreement and predated it.[43] William J. Burns, the Government investigator, traced the Kribs money through the partnership accounts into Mitchell's personal account. Tanner, during the trial, testified that the money from Kribs was taken without Mitchell's knowledge and that Mitchell had cautioned him about using his name in connection with General Land Office work.[44] But Tanner was by then a self-confessed perjurer. Kribs, however, told Detective Burns that the payment to Mitchell and Tanner was merely a matter of convenience.[45]

The falsity of the predated agreement was conclusively proven by Burns, who showed that the paper upon which it was written had not been in use on the Pacific coast until 1903, that the typewriter upon which it had been written had not been in use on the Pacific coast in 1901, and further demonstrated three characteristic misspellings made by young Tanner.[46] Harry C. Robertson, Mitchell's private secretary, also testified as to the original 1901 document.[47]

Mitchell had been warmly greeted in the Senate when he first returned from Oregon in January 1905, but the Senators cooled toward him after Tanner's confession in February. They made no effort to expel him but were no longer cordial.[48] Mitchell retained ex-U.S. Senator John M. Thurston, of Nebraska, as defense counsel.[49] The Government case was the contention that Mitchell had received fees totaling $1,750 paid into the firm of Mitchell & Tanner by Frederick Kribs in violation of the Federal code barring Senators from receiving fees for attention to furthering matters of public business. The Mitchell contention that the money went to the firm and not to him personally was rather conclusively destroyed, while Tanner's testimony that Mitchell knew nothing of the Kribs money did not bear, seemingly, any weight with the jury.

Mitchell did not take the witness stand in his own behalf, as was generally expected.[50] In the closing defense argument, John M. Thurston brushed aside the Government testimony as that of perjurers, pictured Mitchell as the victim of unnamed plotters (although one Mitchell friend named Theodore Roosevelt) and emphasized Mitchell's long public career with particular attention to the appropriations he had obtained for Oregon and to the thousands of favors he had done Oregonians. Thurston described the 70-year-old Mitchell as being "* * * already in the valley, with but a little way for his tottering feet to travel ere he reached the river."[51]

Mitchell was convicted July 5, 1905, sentenced to jail for 6 months, and fined $1,000.[52] Although under pressure to do so, he did not resign from the Senate.[53] He died December 8, 1905, while his conviction was on appeal. The Senate refused to adjourn out of respect to his memory or send a delegation to his funeral.[54]

Judging from the State press comments reprinted in the Oregonian, the majority of Oregon newspapers agreed with the verdict of guilty, but those which did not were vehement in their expression of feeling.

[43] The Oregonian, Feb. 12, 1905.
[44] Ibid., June 25, 1905.
[45] Puter, "Looters of the Public Domain," p. 208.
[46] The Oregonian, Feb. 12, 1905.
[47] Ibid.
[48] Ibid., Feb. 14, 1905.
[49] Ibid., Apr. 30, 1905.
[50] The Oregonian, June 28, 1905.
[51] Ibid., June 30, 1905.
[52] Ibid., July 5, 1905; July 26, 1905.
[53] The Oregonian, Nov. 2, 1905.
[54] The Dictionary of American Biography, XIII, 54.

The Salem Capitol-Journal charged that the Government had "* * * pursued the methods of Russian spies and detectives." It asserted that the jurors had been terrorized by the Government and the press and further asserted that all Senators would be guilty of the same charge.[55] The Gold Beach (Curry County) Globe characterized Mitchell as the noblest mind Oregon ever had.[56]

Mitchell belonged to a passing generation which did not comprehend the change in public temper. He was caught in a shift in public mores, which is a cruel thing. The shift in mores had been long in coming, but was intensified in 1900–1905 with Theodore Roosevelt as President and with the election of Robert M. La Follette, and others of his stamp, to high office. In a long generation after the Civil War, the corporation as an instrument for business was arrogant and irresponsible with the intoxication of undenied success. A large public by 1900 was thoroughly tired of that irresponsibility and wholesale domination of public officials by what the "people" considered the "interests." The wholesale appropriation of the natural resources, "the great barbecue," in the words of Vernon L. Parrington, went swiftly out of style and men like Mitchell whose instincts were of another day were caught up in the change. It is, of course, pure conjecture, but a better defense might have been an honest admission, if he were guilty, of accepting illegal fees. The disposition might then have been to be lenient with the old Senator. In that same summer, there were three trials before the Government could obtain a conviction of Representative John N. Williamson because the jury felt that violation of the land laws was so universal that it would have been discrimination to single out one man for punishment.[57]

Mitchell's attorney realized that the Oregon Senator had been caught in a shift of mores. He said, in an interview printed in the New York Post, that Mitchell was the victim of reform and that Mitchell was no more culpable than certain Eastern senators.

> * * * In the West, eminent men zealous in religion and politics, have abetted these land frauds with the same pride and enthusiasm with which, in the East, gentlemen of similar standing have joined in swindling syndicates, and looting insurance companies.[58]

Oregon was sensitive to the charge that it was less moral than the rest of the Nation. As one Oregon newspaper, already quoted, asserted, all Senators were guilty of Mitchell's offense. John Thurston, his attorney, termed Mitchell an advance agent of prosperity:

> To call Senator Mitchell or Depew a hoary-headed old rascal is both unjust and cruel. Neither of them has inquired too narrowly into the technicalities of law or morals; their eyes have been fixed upon higher things, nobler aims. Each has been devoted to those mighty commercial interests which are the true soul of a commonwealth. Each in his own courageous, though somewhat careless way, has been an advance agent of prosperity.[59]

BLUE MOUNTAIN RESERVE CONSPIRACY

Senator Mitchell was also indicted for participation in the Oregon portion of the Benson-Hyde scheme to control forest reserve boundaries and use the otherwise worthless school sections within contemplated reserves as "base" for the selection of valuable indemnity lands

[55] The Oregonian, July 8, 1905.
[56] Ibid., Aug. 11, 1905.
[57] The Oregonian, Sept. 28, 1905.
[58] The New York Evening Post quoted in the Oregonian, Aug. 28, 1905.
[59] Ibid.

outside the reserves. The "land grabbers" headed, according to Puter's testimony, by Franklin P. Mays, fostered in 1901 the creation of the Blue Mountain Forest Reserve in eastern Oregon.[60] Mays hired the county clerk of Malheur County to circulate a petition for the creation of the forest reserve. He was to be paid $4 per day, but he sublet the contract, so to say, to a bartender in Vale for $2.50 per day. The bartender considerately filled in numerous signatures himself.

The land ring, which included besides Mays, Willard N. Jones and George Sorenson (Jones had once been a partner with Puter and Sorenson and had been indicted but not convicted of an attempt to bribe the U.S. attorney for Oregon to dismiss the Puter indictment), planned to control 200,000 acres within the Blue Mountain Reserve which they would have sold at $5 to $7 an acre as "base" for the purchase of indemnity lands. Also indicted February 13, 1905 were Mitchell, Binger Hermann, and John N. Williamson, Oregon Congressman from Prineville.[61]

There were three convictions; Senator Mitchell was beyond judgment, having died before the trial began. He was to have received 2,000 acres, according to Puter. Actually, the plot was foiled by Roosevelt's dedicated forestry chief, Gifford Pinchot, who was familiar with the technique and carefully drew the Blue Mountain Reserve boundaries to exclude the holdings of the ring.[62]

Mays, Jones, and Sorenson were convicted in September 1906.[63] Mays was sentenced to 4 months in jail and a $10,000 fine, and Jones was sentenced to 8 months. President Taft pardoned Jones and Mays.[64] One ardent Mitchell supporter has alluded to this pardon and asserted that Taft gave the pardon when the record showed the perjured testimony used to convict Jones and Mays.[65] In his "Autobiography," Theodore Roosevelt asserted that his prosecutions without "fear or favor" antagonized the leaders of the Republican Party in Oregon. He charged that half the Oregon delegation to the Republican Convention of 1912 did not vote for him as they had been pledged to do because of the lingering resentment. He charged, too, that the pardon for Mays and Jones was part of the price which the delegation demanded and received for their support to Taft.[66]

TRIALS OF CONGRESSMAN WILLIAMSON

John N. Williamson, Representative in Congress, of Prineville, was indicted for subornation of perjury in February 1905. Williamson and his partners in the sheep business, Dr. Van Gesner, and Marion R. Biggs, U.S. Commissioner in Prineville, were indicted for prevailing upon 45 persons in Prineville to file Timber and Stone Act claims on the even-numbered sections of township 11 south, range 15, east of the Willamette meridian [67] in the "Horse Heaven" country of Crook County. The odd-numbered sections belonged to the Willamette Valley and Cascade Mountain Wagon Road grant and were under

[60] Puter, "Looters of the Public Domain," pp. 347–356.
[61] Puter, "Looters of the Public Domain," p.445.
[62] The Oregonian, Feb. 14, 1905.
[63] Ibid., Sept. 14, 1906.
[64] Scott, "History of the Oregon Country," I, 347.
[65] Galvani, loc. cit., p. 322.
[66] Theodore Roosevelt, "Autobiography" (New York, 1916), p. 388.
[67] The Oregonian, Feb. 12, 1905.

lease to Williamson and Gesner. The land was not really timberland, and the two wished to gain ownership to protect their summer sheep range.[68] Williamson, a partner more than a principal, carried an appeal to the Supreme Court on his congressional immunity to serving a sentence while Congress was in session. The appeal became one of the leading cases on interpretation of the Timber and Stone Act.[69]

There were three trials in the Williamson case. At the third trial in September 1905, all three men were convicted.[70] This is the trial, already mentioned, where the juries in the first trials would not convict because some of the members felt that it would be discrimination to single out individuals for violation of the land laws.

ACQUITTALS OF BINGER HERMANN

Although indicted numerous times, Binger Hermann, the dismissed Commissioner of the General Land Office, was never convicted. He was indicted in Puter's *11–7* case, in the Blue Mountain Reserve case, in the Butte Creek Enclosure case, and once in Washington, D.C., for destroying letter books in the General Land Office before quitting that office on his dismissal.[71] Actually, Hermann appears to have been acting unethically, rather than illegally. His main characteristic seemed to be a willingness to accommodate his friends with any favor he could render. John Isle in "The U.S. Forest Policy" considered Hermann's stand on conservation conscientious, although Lincoln Steffens constantly referred to him as "Hermann the sly."

Puter did not make any big sums of money, for all his scheming. Several instances in his confessions tell how he lost out on big sums. On the 12 claims in *11–7*, he netted $10,000 and all of it went to pay the costs of fraudulent maneuvers. Actually, the real gainers were the timbermen who purchased claims from men like Puter. They paid market price for their lands but received lands they would otherwise not have been allowed to purchase.

DISMISSAL OF NUMEROUS INDICTMENTS

There were numerous cases not treated in this narrative, as it has been confined to the cases involving high public officials. The removal of officers, which began with Commissioner Hermann, penetrated to the local level of the Federal administration. Removed as U.S. Commissioners were: H. W. Reed, J. W. Hamaker, J. O. Hamaker, and Marie Ware. Those removed from district land offices were: Max Whittlesey, E. M. Bratain, F. W. Bartlett, and Asa B. Thompson. Henry Meldrum, surveyor-general or Oregon, was convicted November 17, 1904, for issuing surveying contracts based upon fraudulent requests for survey.[72] Numerous indictments were dropped by the Federal Government in 1908.[73]

[68] *Van Gesner* v. *the United States*, 153 Fed. 54–55.

[69] *Williamson* v. *the United States*, 207 U.S. 425. See p. 75.

[70] The Oregonian, Sept. 28, 1905.

[71] Ibid., Feb. 5, 1905.

[72] Scott, "History of the Oregon Country," I, 346–48.

[73] The Oregonian, Aug. 3, 1908. Many interesting details have necessarily been omitted from this recital. They may be found in Lincol Steffens, "The Taming of the West," American Magazine, LXIV (1907), 489–505, 585–602. For those with access to the Oregon Collection in the University of Oregon Library, the three large scrapbooks of W. G. Steel are a convenient source to the newspaper accounts of the Mitchell trial. Puter's "Looters of the Public Domain" is valuable for its details on the complicated techniques of land fraud.

The vigorous prosecutions seemingly had accomplished their purpose in halting wholesale fraud in acquiring public lands. In the tradition of the "muckraking" era, and in the antimonopoly tradition of American life, the part fraud has played in the disposition of the public lands has possibly been overemphasized, although the fact is clear that thousands of men, many of them in high offices, practiced land fraud, seemingly with a clear conscience. The conviction of a patriarchal U.S. Senator from Oregon, however, was due notice that the "great barbecue" was over.

CHAPTER X

THE HOMESTEAD ACT AND AFTER

The Homestead Act, in terms of the acreage, has been far and away the most important of the land acts which governed the disposition of the public domain in Oregon; sales for cash follow in importance. Over one-third of the land transferred in Oregon was under the Homestead Act.

Although the most active use of the Homestead Act was in the decade 1910–19, the decade of greatest land transference by all means was that of 1900–1909, which was marked by a timberland buying boom. In that decade, 6,910,135 acres were transferred, exclusive of the State grant and the railroad grants, to private ownership. The 40 years from 1890 to 1930 were the most important in terms of acreage. In those decades the totals were more than 2 million acres in each decade. The most important 20 years was that period between 1890 and 1910, when approximately one-third of the total, 10,595,237 acres, was patented to individuals. The peak year was 1903, when 1,616,131 acres were patented from the public domain.

Oregonians naturally welcomed the enactment in 1862 of the long-demanded Homestead Act. Oregon residents thought it should have been passed 20 years previously and they assigned the reason for this failure to Southern politicians who despised "small fisted farmers living on a quarter section.[1] A letter in the Oregonian at the time of the enactment offered the opinion that its purpose was to provide that every head of a family—

> * * * might have a spot of land, that the God of Nature has made for his children, that they may cultivate for their own.[2]

The Oregonian, a Republican paper, was intensely proud that the Homestead Act was an achievement of the Republican Party.

> This great national measure * * * designed to secure to all what is necessary for the highest development of our minds, it should be remembered, was consummated in the second year of the administration of Abraham Lincoln.[3]

Disposition to individuals by decades

(Acres)

1870–79	384, 130	1910–19	3, 244, 182
1880–89	2, 189, 180	1920–29	2, 645, 414
1890–99	3, 685, 102	1930–39	575, 156
1900–1909	6, 910, 135	1940–49	77, 731

Source: Computed from "Senate Documents," 58th Cong., 3d sess., No. 189, and statistics furnished by the Bureau of Land Management.

TWENTIETH CENTURY HOMESTEADING

The Homestead Act was passed in 1862, but its years of greatest use in Oregon were in the 20th century. The decade 1910–19 was the

[1] The Oregonian, Oct. 1, 1859.
[2] Ibid., Aug 18, 1862.
[3] Ibid., July 30, 1862.

most important in Oregon in terms of final homestead entries. In that decade 2,873,183 acres were taken under the homestead system. On first thought one might not think the decade 1920–29 important in homestead history; yet it ranked closely behind 1910–19 as the second most important decade, when 2,517,588 acres were taken under its provisions. As the following chart will indicate, in the 40 years from 1890–1930, the rate did not drop below 1 million acres per decade.

Final homestead entries

Total acreage by decades:	
1870–79	383, 853
1880–89	816, 149
1890–99	1, 600, 778
1900–1909	1, 676, 897
1910–19	2, 873, 183
1920–29	2, 517, 558
1930–39	557, 412
Total acreage by decades—Continued	
1940–49	69, 936
Commuted homestead entries:	
1882–89	94, 952
1890–99	158, 290
1900–1904	334, 771

Source: Commuted homesteads, homesteads where the entryman elected to pay $1.25 per acre in place of living on the homestead the required time, are included in the totals after 1904. Computed from ' Senate Documents," 59th Cong., 3d sess., No. 189, and unpublished statistics furnished by the Bureau of Land Management.

The Donation Act had taken up the most arable land in the Willamette, Rogue, and Umpqua valleys. The Homestead Act was important in the settlement of eastern Oregon and in the further settlement of western Oregon. The commutation clause of the Homestead Act, which authorized sale for cash in lieu of the residence requirements, lent itself to the needs of timberland buyers and its use was a feature of the timber boom of 1900–1910.

Free land, that is, land which could be procured by settlement and nominal fees, possibly invited rapid settlement upon land inherently incapable of supporting the homestead principle, a principle shattered on the marginal lands of eastern Oregon. The railroads which penetrated central Oregon about 1910 fostered a land boom in eastern Oregon. The hopes of people may have been too high, and certainly the promotion "literature" overestimated, to put it most kindly, the ease with which raw land could be transformed into productive land. The disappointment which failure must have bred can be read in the statistics and seen on the land.

ORIGINAL AND FINAL ENTRY

The figures already quoted are those of final entries, those which passed to patent. The original entry and final entry tabulations tell part of the story of the breakdown of the homestead principle. Between 1905 and 1950, there were 7,016,350 acres in final entries. The original entries covered 11,608,683 acres. There is a saying in the West that a homesteader bet his time against the Government's land and in Oregon the Government won back 4,593,333 acres. In 1920 there were 999,608 acres in original entries. In normal course they would have passed to patent in 1923 when 313,984 acres passed to final entry.

Original homestead entries

1905–9	1, 764, 830
1910–19	5, 380, 780
1920–29	3, 705, 528
1930–39	751, 009
1940–49	6, 446

Source: From statistics furnished by the Bureau of Land Management.

The American occupation of the continental domain was not, in any sense, a "planned" occupation. It was a mass movement of self-governing people who saw an opportunity to carry their institutions to new lands. Tremendous energy was expended in that movement, and there was undoubtedly much trial and error in its methods. The large discrepancy between original and final entries was a part of that trial and error, for the American in Oregon was free to make a good choice of homestead; he was free also to make a bad choice.

The commuted homestead was a favored means of acquiring timber land. The Oregon timber land boom is reflected in the statistics covering the commuted homestead. In the years 1900–1904, twice as much acreage was commuted as in the preceding 10 years. From 1890–99 there were 158,306 commuted acres. From 1900–1904 there 334,771 commuted acres. After 1904 the commuted acreage was carried in the general homestead total so that it is difficult to know the exact importance of the commuted homestead in acquiring land.

CASH SALES

The Federal Government was selling land before it gave it away by the Homestead Act, and it continued to sell land after the Homestead Act. It sold it through the provisions of such acts as the Timber and Stone Act, which authorized the sale of timber land at a minimum of $2.50 per acre. It sold land at public auction. Land left unsold after auction was open to private entry at a minimum of $1.25 per acre. That this sale and that the granting of land to railroads should have continued after passage of the Homestead Act has been roundly criticized, notably by Paul Wallace Gates.[4] He makes an excellent case for this in the Mississippi Valley, but his statement that the most fertile parts of Oregon were open to cash purchase after the enactment of the Homestead Act [5] is not borne out by the facts of Oregon settlement. The Donation Act of 1850 had provided for the settlement of the lands which at the time were considered the finest lands in Oregon. The cash system did compete with the homestead system in eastern Oregon, but it was also complementary to it. In the 20th century, as Gates noted, cash sales were a means of acquiring timber land which was really not suitable for settlement.

Actually, it might have been the better part of wisdom to have sold the eastern Oregon land for a cash price, which would have forestalled some of the disappointments of homesteading marginal lands.

By 1904, 4,211,483 acres had been sold for cash.[6] The acreage for figures for cash sales from 1904 to 1950 are not available. The monetary returns were $346,119. Assuming the Government minimum of $1.25 per acre, the $346,119 would indicate that 276,959 acres were sold for cash at public auction or by private entry following public auction. This calculation does not include lands sold for cash under the Timber and Stone Act and Desert Lands Act. The Timber and Stone Act accounted for 1,875,097 acres; the Desert Lands Act, for 250,111 acres. Added to the pre-1904 total this would indicate that 6,455,551 acres were sold under the major acts providing for cash sale.

---

[4] "The Homestead Law in an Incongruous Land System," The American Historical Review, XLI (1935-36), 652-682.
[5] Ibid., p. 660.
[6] S. Doc. No. 189 (58th Cong., 3d sess.), p. 208.

RAILROAD GRANTS

Only 1,588,532 acres of Oregon land has been conveyed by railroad grants, but this in itself does not indicate the role of the railroad land grants in Oregon. When the Southern Pacific owned the Oregon and California grant, it was the biggest owner of timberland in the United States. However, the Southern Pacific lost 2,890,893 acres of the original 3,728,000 acres because of violation of the granting terms.[7] Previous to the forfeiture, 837,107 acres had been patented to the railroad and sold by it.

The Northern Pacific grant was responsible for conveying 751,425 acres to private ownership. A very small portion of the Northern Pacific grant was in Oregon, but the operation of several forest lieu acts of 1897–1899 which authorized the Northern Pacific, among others, to trade its land within forest reserve boundaries for land outside the boundaries, made the Northern Pacific grant the "base" for locating Oregon timberland.[8]

Local resentment in Oregon and in the West was aroused by the possession of vacant lands by railroad corporations. The resentment was an expression of the feeling that the land grants held back development and fostered an undemocratic monopoly in land. The presence of a land grant did work certain hardships upon local inhabitants. The lands within the limits of a railroad grant were withdrawn from settlement pending survey and determination of which sections belonged to the railroads. Once land was withdrawn from settlement, the railroads never hurried to claim patent, for that would have placed the land on the local tax roll. Instead, the railroad would not apply for a patent until it had a purchaser for a tract. This naturally hampered settlement.

Railroad grants were unpopular in Oregon, especially the Oregon and California grant when the Southern Pacific refused to sell any more land. Yet Harvey W. Scott, editor of the Oregonian, and no friend of any action which would imperil Oregon development, has left a balanced judgment on the railroad grants. In 1888 he wrote:

> We hear a good deal about "our wasted public heritage." Large bodies of land have been given to corporations chiefly for the construction of railroads * * *. When it began, many years ago, public land was very abundant * * *.
>
> It is easy, now, for anyone to say that so much land ought not to have been given away to railroad corporations, for nothing is more natural, since the country has obtained the railroads it desired, than to wish the Government had the land back again.

Earlier, in 1883, he had written:

> * * * The railroads have obtained land enough, and in many cases more than enough; but there is no point whatever in losing sight of the circumstances under which the lands were given. Nor is there candor or good sense in pretending that the results have not been, on the whole, highly advantageous to the country. It is particularly uncandid to parade the present value of the lands—which value has been almost wholly created * * * by the railroads—as proof that * * * the people have been "robbed of an imperial domain." The truth is, the people were anxious to get the railroads even at the sacrifice of large bodies of the public lands, and they would pursue the same policy under similar circumstances.[9]

[7] Ch. V.
[8] Ch. VIII.
[9] Scott, "History of the Oregon Country," IV, 252, 255.

LANDOWNERSHIP PATTERN

Despite fears to the contrary, the disposition of the public lands in Oregon has resulted in no land monoply and the ownership has accommodated itself to the requirements of land holdings in lumbering, farming, and ranching. There is a concentration of ownership in timberlands, but it is balanced by thousands of small timber holdings. In the arable valleys are the family-sized farms of the homestead ideal and in eastern Oregon the ranches are larger, in keeping with the demands of a pastoral life. As nationally, so in Oregon, the disposition of the public domain, despite evasion of intent, despite outright fraud, has confirmed the belief of Lincoln when he said:

> It has long been the cherished opinion of some of our wisest statesmen that the people of the United States had a higher and more enduring interest in the early settlement and substantial cultivation of the public lands than in the amount of direct revenue to be derived from the sale of them.[10]

[10] James D. Richardson, "A Compilation of the Messages and Papers of the Presidents" (New York, VI, 186.

SUMMARY

The State of Oregon, where the Willamette Valley was settled by the first Americans to migrate to the old Oregon country, has a land area of 61 million acres. After the British withdrawal in 1846, except for a vague Indian title, the title to these acres rested with the Government of the United States. In 100 years, 29 million acres have been transferred from public to private ownership. This is approximately one-half the land of Oregon, and by all odds the most immediately important half. It includes the farms of the western valleys, the ranches of eastern Oregon, and 11 million of the choice timbered acres of the 28 million forested acres in Oregon.

The disposition of this public domain began in 1850, reached a climax in the 1st decade of the 20th century, and by 1950 was practically completed. There are unique features to the transfer of public land in Oregon. The Donation Land Act, which was a precursor of the national Homestead Act, provided, in 1850, for as much as 640 acres per family as an award for migrating to Oregon. Two million acres of the open valley land of western Oregon were taken up under its terms.

The Oregon & California Railroad was granted a 3,728,000-acre subsidy for construction of a railroad between Portland and the California boundary, where its tracks connected with the California & Oregon Railroad constructed north from Sacramento. The grant was authorized in 1866; the construction was completed in 1887. In 1916, some 2,890,000 acres of the grant were revested by the United States, because the Southern Pacific, a subsequent owner of the grant, sold lands in units larger than 160 acres and at a price in excess of $2.50 per acre, all in explicit violation of the grant terms. The lands still retain their identity and are administered at present as the Oregon & California revested lands by the Bureau of Land Management, although approximately 500,000 acres are administered by the Forest Service as national forest lands.

The Congress authorized, by several acts in the 1860's, land grants for the construction of wagon roads in Oregon. There had been wagon-road grants previous to the Oregon grants, but the 2,490,000 acres granted in Oregon account for two-thirds of all land granted for wagon roads. The United States revested 93,000 acres from the Coos Bay Wagon Road Co. for violation of the granting act by sales in excess of 160 acres and a $2.50 per acre maximum price.

The State of Oregon itself has been a major recipient of public lands. It has received 4,329,435 acres under the various acts authorizing grants to the States. Of this, 4,035,000 acres have been for the support of education. One-third of the State grant was sold during a timberland boom between 1900 and 1910 when the school lands became a favorite means of timberland buyers who wished to purchase land in large tracts.

Oregon has 28 million acres in its forests. In western Oregon the timber is predominantly Douglas-fir. In eastern Oregon there are scattered forests of ponderosa pine. Private ownership controls 11 million of the best of these acres. The bulk of this private holding was extracted from the public domain at the turn of the 20th century.

When the timberland of the Great Lakes States had been logged, the timber barons moved their operations west to the Pacific Northwest and California. Oregon, with the greatest stumpage per acre, was the object of special attention by timberland brokers. Timberland was acquired in many ways. It was purchased outright for cash. It was obtained through the Homestead Act, particularly under the commutation clause which permitted the substitution of cash for the residence requirement. The Timber and Stone Act, which authorized sale of timberland in 160-acre units at $2.50 per acre, was a ready means for acquiring timberland.

The commuted homestead and the Timber and Stone Act offered timberland in small units. Larger tracts were desirable and other laws furnished means to acquire timberland by the thousands of acres. Purchase of the State indemnity lands was one such means. The operation of several forest lieu acts fostered a concentration in Oregon timberland ownership. The various lieu acts authorized holders of perfected and unperfected claims within the national forest reserves to exchange them for land outside the reserves. These acts made the claims, particularly the sections of the Northern Pacific land grant, "base" for the selection of timberland in large blocks. The Northern Pacific sold its "lieu" rights to timber brokers who used the scrip to acquire ownership of large blocks of timberland.

The Oregon & California Railroad grant, which checkerboards western Oregon, contains 60 billion feet of timber, 50 billion on the portion now administered by the Bureau of Land Management and 10 billion on the portion administered by the Forest Service. When the Southern Pacific owned the grant, it was the greatest owner of timberland in the Nation. The sales which brought its ultimate revestment to the United States were sales of timberlands in larger units and at a higher price than the granting act authorized. The wagon-road grants, mentioned earlier, were also a source of timberland.

Despite the massive holdings of such giants of the timber industry as the Weyerhaeuser Timber Co., there is a not inconsequential number of small holdings. The small 160-acre units were acquired under the Homestead Act and the Timber and Stone Act. The concentrations of large holdings were acquired through the railroad and wagon-road grants, purchase of State lands, and the purchase of small holdings.

Fraudulent means of acquiring land, particularly timberland, was brought to a high degree of "art" by "land sharks." Fraudulent acquisition of timberland, however, was dealt a hard blow in 1905 by the conviction in Federal court of the senior Senator from Oregon, John H. Mitchell, for complicity in the fraudulent patenting of public lands. Another public official convicted was John N. Williamson, Congressman from Prineville, although his congressional position was coincidental with his land dealings. Although under numerous indictments, the other Oregon Representative in Congress, Binger Hermann, was never convicted. Hermann had been dismissed in 1902 as Commissioner of the General Land Office. He returned to Oregon where he was elected to Congress. It was this election of Hermann which is generally credited with concentrating land-fraud prosecutions in Oregon. The Theodore Roosevelt administration was nettled that

Hermann should be returned to public office and seemingly concentrated its attentions on discrediting him in his own State.

Senator Mitchell was convicted on the evidence furnished by Stephen A. Douglas Puter, whose book, "Looters of the Public Domain," sustains his claim to being "king of the Oregon land fraud ring." Puter was convicted in December 1904 of land fraud covering 12 fraudulent homestead entries in township 11, range 7, east of the Willamette meridian. After his conviction he asserted that Senator Mitchell had accepted money from him to expedite the patenting of the 12 fraudulent claims. This evidence could not be substantiated. Puter then offered the information to Francis J. Heney, special assistant to the Attorney General of the United States prosecuting the Oregon land frauds, that Frederick A. Kribs, a timber broker, had paid Mitchell for services by check. The Senator was indicted and convicted upon this charge. He died before his appeal was heard by the higher courts. His conviction served notice that the day of wholesale land fraud in acquisition of public lands was closed. There were numerous other indictments and convictions in Oregon at the same time, but in 1908 the Government dismissed many of the remaining indictments, seemingly satisfied that the prosecution of Puter, Mitchell, and Hermann had ended the wholesale practice of land fraud.

Although little may be written from official documents about it except for statistical material, the Homestead Act has been the most important means of transferring land to private ownership. Some 11 million acres passed from the public domain under the homestead system. Sale for cash was second in importance with some 6 million acres. The most important decade for the homestead system, in terms of acreage, was that between 1910–19, when 2,873,183 acres was patented; closely followed by the decade 1920–29, when 2,517,588 acres were patented.

Despite early fears that the land policy would promote land monopoly, no such monopoly appeared in Oregon. The ownership pattern has accommodated itself to the landholding needs of Oregon. In western Oregon are the family-sized farms of the ideal homestead; in eastern Oregon the ranches are larger, in keeping with the needs of a pastoral life. There is a concentration of ownership of timberlands, probably necessary and desirable for the practice of good forestry, but even in timber ownership there are thousands of 160-acre holdings, reflecting again the operation of the homestead principle.

The major modes of disposition have resulted in the following distribution of the grand total.

Disposition of the public domain in Oregon [1]

	Acres		Acres
Homestead	11, 097, 982	Wagon-road grants	2, 490, 890
Sales	6, 455, 551	Railroad grants	1, 588, 532
Grant to State	4, 329, 445	Miscellaneous	992, 921
Donation claims	2, 614, 082		
		Total	29, 569, 403

[1] These totals have been computed from statistics in "Senate Documents," 58th Cong., 3d sess., No. 189, and from a recapitulation of Oregon figures furnished by the Bureau of Land Management.

APPENDIX

Indian Cession Treaties in Oregon

To acquire these cessions the United States paid some $973,650. These sums were not turned over to the tribes in cash, but were distributed in annual installments of goods, provisions, and equipment. This figure is an approximation, determined by the cash amounts provided in the treaties. It does not account for expenditures contracted by the United States for erecting buildings and performing services toward integrating the Indians with the civilization which overcame them.

The treaties also provided reservations for the tribes. The reservations as established by treaty or Executive order with their acreages as of 1880 were:

	Acres
Grande Ronde (western Oregon)	61, 440
Klamath (southeastern Oregon)	1, 056, 000
Malheur (southeastern Oregon)	1, 778, 560
Siletz (Oregon coast)	225, 000
Umatilla (northeastern Oregon)	268, 800
Warm Springs (central Oregon)	464, 000

The Malheur Reservation is no longer in existence. The acreage figures are from Thomas Donaldson, "The Public Domain, Its History with Statistics" (Washington, 1881), p. 247.

The following treaties are cited as they appear in the Statutes at Large. They may be conveniently seen in Charles J. Kappler, editor and compiler, "Indian Affairs, Laws and Treaties" (Washington, 1903). The numerals in parentheses refer to the tracts as outlined in plate 51, Bureau of Ethnology, eighteenth annual report, II.

1. Rogue Rivers, September 10, 1853; ratified April 12, 1854; proclaimed February 5, 1855. A $60,000 payment in goods and farm implements, with $15,000 to be withheld by the Government to pay claims arising from the Rogue War. An added $15,000 provided when the Rogue River Tribe moved from the Table Rock Reserve (312). Statutes at Large, X, 1018.
2. Umpqua (Cow Creek Band), September 19, 1853; ratified April 12, 1854; proclaimed February 5, 1855. Payment, $12,000 (313). Ibid., X, 1122.
3. Chastas [Shastas], November 18, 1854; ratified March 3, 1855; proclaimed April 10, 1855. Payment, $36,000 (343). Ibid., 1122.
4. Umpquas and Calapooias, November 29, 1854; ratified March 3, 1855; proclaimed March 30, 1855. Payment, $40,000 with an additional $10,000 for expenses of moving to a reservation (344). Ibid., 1125.
5. Calapooias and Confederated Bands of the Willamette Valley, January 22, 1855; ratified March 3, 1855; proclaimed April 10, 1855. Payment, $165,000 (352). Ibid., 1143.
6. Walla Walla, Cayuse, and Umatilla, June 9, 1855; ratified March 9, 1859; proclaimed April 11, 1859. Partly in Washington. Payment, $100,000 (362). Ibid., XII, 945.
7. Nez Perce, June 11, 1855; ratified March 9, 1859; proclaimed April 29, 1859. Payment, $200,000. Greatest portion of cession was in Idaho. A proviso was included to keep those who drank "ardent spirits" from sharing in the annuities (366). Ibid., 957.

8. Confederated Bands of Middle Oregon, June 25, 1855; ratified March 8, 1859; proclaimed April 18, 1959. Payment, $100,000 (369). Ibid., 963.

9. Oregon Coast Tribes, several unratified treaties negotiated between August 11, 1855, and September 8, 1855 (397, 479, 578, 579).

10. Molala, December 21, 1855; ratified March 8, 1859; proclaimed April 29, 1859. Payment of $12,000 to purchase claims of settlers on the Grande Ronde Reservation and the Molalas to share the settlement made with the Calapooias and Umpquas (401). Ibid., 981.

11. Nez Perce, June 9, 1863; ratified April 7, 1867; proclaimed April 20, 1867. A cession of a portion of the reservation created by earlier treaty. The United States to pay for improvements upon ceded land. Payment, $262,500. Cession in Washington, Oregon, and Idaho (441). Ibid., XIV, 647.

12. Klamath, Modocs and Yahooskin Band Snakes, October 14, 1864; ratified with amendments July 2, 1866; amendments agreed to December 10, 1869; proclaimed February 10, 1870. Partly in California. Payment, $80,000 expended "to promote well being of the Indians, advance them in civilization and especially agriculture, and to secure their moral improvement and education" (462). Ibid., XV, 707.

13. Snakes (Woll-pah-pe band), August 12, 1865; ratified July 5, 1866; proclaimed July 10, 1866. Overlaps the Klamath cession. Payment, $27,000 (474). Ibid., XIV, 683.

BIBLIOGRAPHY

A. Bibliographical Aids

Judson, Katharine Berry. "Subject Index to the History of the Pacific Northwest and of Alaska As Found in the United States Government Documents 1789–1881." Olympia, Washington, 1913.

Rowe, Howard Marshall. "A Preliminary Draft of a Subject Index to Historical Material of the Pacific Northwest and Alaska To Be Found in the United States Congressional Series and Other United States Public Documents from 1881–1931." Unpublished master's thesis, University of Idaho, 1938.

B. Manuscripts

Business Correspondence of William Hawks and George S. Canfield, 1902–3. Oregon Collection, University of Oregon Library.

Statistics 1905–50 furnished by Bureau of Land Management February 17, 1951.

C. Federal Documents

Statutes at Large, 1789–1949. 63 vols. Boston, 1845–73; Washington, 1873–1949.

Kappler, Charles J., comp. "Indian Affairs, Laws and Treaties." Washington, 1903. Also published in "Senate Documents," 57th Cong., 1st sess., No. 452.

CONGRESSIONAL DOCUMENTS

The Journals of the Continental Congress (Library of Congress edition). 34 vols. Washington, 1904–1937.

The Annals of the Congress of the United States, 18 Cong., 1st sess.

Register of the Debates in Congress, 18th Cong., 2d sess.

The Congressional Globe:
- 27th Cong., 3d sess.
- 28th Cong., 1st sess.
- 29th Cong., 1st sess.
- 31st Cong., 1st sess.
- 38th Cong., 1st sess.
- 39th Cong., 1st sess.
- 39th Cong., 2d sess.
- 40th Cong., 3d sess.
- 41st Cong., 1st sess.
- 41st Cong., 2d sess.

The Congressional Record:
- 48th Cong., 1st sess.
- 49th Cong., 1st sess.
- 58th Cong., 3d sess.
- 59th Cong., 2d sess.
- 64th Cong., 1st sess.

Senate executive documents:
- 31st Cong., 2d sess., No. 1.
- 34th Cong., 1st sess., No. 26.
- 35th Cong., 2d sess., No. 32.
- 50th Cong., 1st sess., No. 124.
- 50th Cong., 1st sess., No. 161.

Senate documents:
- 58th Cong., 3d sess., No. 189.
- 60th Cong., 2d sess., No. 676, part 2.
- 62d Cong., 1st sess., No. 27.
- 62d Cong., 3d sess., No. 1097.
- 65th Cong., 1st sess., No. 35.

Senate miscellaneous documents: 30th Cong., 1st sess., No. 142.

Senate reports:
41st Cong., 1st sess., No. 3.
49th Cong., 1st sess., No. 1088.
83d Cong., 2d sess., No. 1631.
85th Cong., 2d sess., No. 1518.
House executive documents:
34th Cong., 1st sess., No. 93.
34th Cong., 3d sess., No. 1, part 2.
35th Cong., 1st sess., No. 39.
35th Cong., 1st sess., No. 112.
35th Cong., 2d sess., No. 2, part 2.
House miscellaneous documents:
30th Cong., 1st sess., No. 29.
41st Cong., 3d sess., No. 20.
House reports:
31st Cong., 1st sess., No. 271.
46th Cong., 3d sess., No. 332.
49th Cong., 1st sess., No. 931.
60th Cong., 1st sess., No. 1301.
64th Cong., 1st sess., No. 623.
83d Cong., 2d sess., No. 2483.
85th Cong., 2d sess., No. 2278.
85th Cong., 2d sess., No. 2544.

EXECUTIVE REPORTS

Bureau of Ethnology. Eighteenth Annual Report. 3 vols. Washington, 1899.
General Land Office, Report, 1886, 1888, 1925.
Report of the Director of the Bureau of Land Management, 1950, Statistical Appendix.
Secretary of the Interior, Report. 1904, 1906, 1908.

LEGAL CASES

Alsea Band of Tillamooks et. al. v. *U.S.*, 103 Ct. of Claims 497; 115 Ct. of Claims 463; 71 S. Ct. 552.
Gesner v. *U.S.*, 153 Fed. 54.
Oregon and California Railroad v. *U.S.*, 238 U.S. 407.
Southern Oregon Company v. *U.S.*, 241 Fed. 16.
U.S. v. *Budd*, 144 U.S. 154.
U.S. v. *California and Oregon Land Company*, 192 U.S. 357.
U.S. v. *The Dalles Military Road Company*, 40 Fed. 114.
U.S. v. *Klamath and Moadoc* [Modoc] *Tribes of Indians*, 304 U.S. 119.
U.S. v. *Oregon and California Railroad*, 8 Fed. (2d) 645.
U.S. v. *Oregon Central Military Road Company*, 40 Fed. 120.
U.S. v. *Willamette Valley and Cascade Mountain Wagon Road Company*, 42 Fed. 352.

D. Federal Publications

Bureau of the Census. Historical Statistics of the United States, 1789–1945. Washington, 1949.
Bureau of the Census. Sixteenth Census, Population I.
———. Seventeenth Census, Preliminary Count, Series 2, No. 5; Series 3, No. 2.
———. Statistical Abstract of the United States, 1950. Washington, 1950.
Bureau of Corporations. The Lumber Industry. 3 vols. Washington, 1913–14.
Donaldson, Thomas. The Public Domain, Its History With Statistics. Washington, 1883.
Forest Service. Gauging the Timber Resource of the United States. Washington, 1946.
———. The Management Status of the Forest Lands of the United States. Washington, 1946.
———. Timber Depletion, Lumber Prices, Lumber Export and Concentration of Ownership. Washington, 1938.
———. Timber Resources for America's Future. Washington, 1958.
General Land Office. Land of the Free. Washington, 1938.
———. Forever Timber. [Portland, Oregon], n.d.
National Resources Committee. Forest Resources of the Pacific Northwest. Washington, 1938.

E. Oregon Documents

Desert Land Board. Second Biennial Report, 1913.
———. Third Biennial Report, 1915.
General Laws of Oregon. 1860, 1866, 1868, 1870, 1878, 1887, 1895, 1899, 1903, 1907.
Grover, Lafayette, comp. The Archives of Oregon: Including the Journals, Governor's Messages, and Public Papers of Oregon. Salem, 1853.
State Land Agent. First Biennial Report. 1896.
———. Fifth Biennial Report. 1905.
———. Sixth Biennial Report. 1907.
State Land Board. Biennial Report. 1880, 1884, 1886, 1905.

F. Newspapers

The Oregonian. 1859, 1862, 1869–71, 1873, 1874, 1876–78, 1882, 1900, 1904–08, 1910, 1947. Portland.
Oregon Spectator. 1846–48, 1850–51. Oregon City.
Daily Union. 1872. Sacramento, Calif.

G. Collected Documents and Reference Works

Johnson, Allen and Malone, Dumas, eds. The Dictionary of American Biography. 31 vols. New York, 1931.
Oregon Pioneer Association. Transactions. 1873.
Richardson, James D., comp. A Compilation of the Messages and Papers of the Presidents, 1789–1899. 10 vols. New York, 1899.
Scott, Harvey W. History of the Oregon Country. 6 vols. Cambridge, Mass., 1924.

H. Reminiscences and Autobiography

Benton, Thomas H. Thirty Years' View. 2 vols. New York, 1854.
Burnett, Peter H. Recollections and Opinions of an Old Pioneer. New York, 1880.
Nash, Wallis. Two Years in Oregon. New York, 1882.
Puter, S. A. D., and Stevens, Horace. Looters of the Public Domain. Portland, 1908.
Roosevelt, Theodore. Autobiography. New York, 1916.

I. Monographs and Special Studies

Amundson, Carroll. "History of the Willamette Valley and Cascade Mountain Wagon Road Company." University of Oregon Thesis Series No. 17. [Eugene, 1942].
Bruce, H. S. "A History of the Oregon Central Military Wagon Road Company, With Reference to the Histories of Four Other Land Grand Companies in the State of Oregon." Unpublished master's thesis, University of Oregon, 1936.
"Bunyan in Broadcloth: The House of Weyerhaeuser," Fortune, IX, 63–65, 170–182 (April 1934).
Coan, C. F. "The First Stage of the Federal Indian Policy in the Pacific Northwest, 1849–52." Oregon Historical Quarterly, XXII, 46–89 (1921).
Davenport, T. W. "An Object Lesson in Paternalism," Oregon Historical Quarterly, IV, 33–54 (1903).
Davis, H. L. "Back to the Land—Oregon 1907," American Mercury, XVI, 314–323 (1929).
Douglas, Jesse. "Origins of the Population of Oregon in 1850," Pacific Northwest Quarterly, XLI, 95–108 (1950).
Dunham, Harold Hathaway. Government Handout: A Study in the Administration of the Public Lands, 1875–91. Ann Arbor, 1941.
Ellis, David Maldwyn. "The Oregon California Land Grant 1866–1945," Pacific Northwest Quarterly, XXXIX, 253–383 (1948).
Galvani, William H. "Recollections of J. F. Stevens and Senator Mitchell," Oregon Historical Quarterly, XLIV, 313–326 (1943).
Ganoe, John Tilson. "The History of the Oregon and California Railroad," Oregon Historical Quarterly, XXV, 236–283, 330–352 (1926).
Gates, Paul Wallace. "The Homestead Law in an Incongruous Land System," American Historical Review, XLI, 152–182 (1935–36).

Haney, Lewis Henry. A Congressional History of Railways, 1850–1887, Bulletin University of Wisconsin No. 342. Madison, 1910.

Hawk, Ray Norman. "A History of the Irreducible School Fund in Oregon." Unpublished doctoral dissertation, University of Oregon, 1949.

Hedges, James B. "Promotion of Immigration to Pacific Northwest by Railroads," Mississippi Valley Historical Review, XV, 183–203 (1928).

Holman, Frederick V. "A Brief History of the Oregon Provisional Government and What Caused Its Formation," Oregon Historical Quarterly, XIII, 89–139 (1912).

Hoopes, Alban W. Indian Affairs and Their Administration. Philadelphia, 1932.

Ise, John. The United States Forest Policy. New Haven, 1920.

Jacobs, Melvin Clay. Winning Oregon: A Study of an Expansionist Movement. Caldwell, Idaho, 1938.

Lillard, Richard G. "Timber King," Pacific Spectator, I, 14–27 (1947).

Martig, Ralph. "Hudson's Bay Company Claims, 1846–69," Oregon Historical Quarterly, XXXVI, 60–70 (1935).

Merk, Frederick. "Oregon Pioneers and the Boundary," American Historical Review, XXIX, 681–699 (1923).

Mills, Randall V. Railroads Down the Valleys: Some Short Lines of the Oregon Country. Palo Alto, Calif., 1950.

Moores, Charles B. "The Donation Land Law," The Oregonian, December 4, 1900.

Oliphant, James Orin. "The Range Cattle Industry in the Oregon Country to 1890." Unpublished doctoral dissertation, Harvard University, 1930.

Orfield, Mathias Nordberg. Federal Land Grants to the States with Special Reference to Minnesota, University of Minnesota Studies in Social Sciences No. 2. Minneapolis, 1915.

Peffer, E. Louise. The Closing of the Public Domain. Disposal and Reservation Policies 1900–50. Stanford, Calif., 1951.

Salo, Sarah Jenkins. Timber Concentration in the Pacific Northwest with Special Reference to the Timber Holdings of the Southern Pacific, the Northern Pacific Railroad and the Weyerhaeuser Timber Company. Ann Arbor, 1945.

Scott, Harvey W. "The Pioneer Character of Oregon Progress," Oregon Historical Quarterly, XVIII, 345–395 (1917).

Shippee, Lester Burrell. "The Federal Relations of Oregon," Oregon Historical Quarterly, XX, 345–395 (1919).

Smith, Warren D. "Physical and Economic Geography of Oregon," Commonwealth Review, VII, 56–89 (1924).

Snow, Charles MacC. "A History of Oregon Land Grants." Unpublished bachelor's thesis, University of Oregon, 1909.

Steffens, Lincoln. "The Making of a Fighter," American Magazine, LXIV, 339–356 (1907).

———. "The Taming of the West," American Magazine, LXIV, 489–505, 585–602 (1907).

Stephenson, George M. The Political History of the Public Lands from 1840–62. Boston, 1917.

Strong, Dexter K. "Beef Cattle Industry in Oregon, 1890–1938," Oregon Historical Quarterly, XLI, 251–287 (1940).

Thurston, Samuel Royal. "Diary of Samuel Royal Thurston," Oregon Historical Quarterly, XV, 153–205 (1914).

Victor, F. F. "Our Public Land System and Its Relation to Education," Oregon Historical Quarterly, I, 132–157 (1899).

Vinnedge, Robert W. The Pacific Northwest Lumber Industry and Its Development, Yale University Lumber Series No. 4. New Haven, 1920.

Whitesmith, Benjamin MacLean. "Henry Villard and the Development of Oregon," University of Oregon Thesis Series No. 14 [Eugene, 1940].

Wolf, Ray O. "A History of Oregon School Lands 1849–1900." Unpublished master's thesis, University of Oregon, 1940.

Young, F. G. "Financial History of the State of Oregon," Oregon Historical Quarterly, X, 366–384; XI, 121–161 (1909-10).

J. Pamphlets

Deschutes Irrigation Company. Government Carey Act Irrigation Land in the Deschutes Valley Central Oregon. N.p. [1908]. In Bancroft Library, University of California.

Great Northern Railway. Oregon—320 Acres Free. N.p. [1910].

———. Uncle Sam Opens 1800 Farm Homes for Settlers in Central Oregon. N.p. [1914]. In Bancroft Library, University of California.

Oregon and Western Colonization Company. Military Road Grant Lands 800,000 Acres in Central Oregon. St. Paul, n.d. In Bancroft Library, University of California.

Southern Pacific. Oregon for the Settler. Portland, n.d. In San Francisco Public Library.

K. General Works

Bailey, Thomas A. A Diplomatic History of the American People, 3d edition. New York, 1946.

Bancroft, Hubert Howe. Works. 39 vols. San Francsico, 1886–1890.

Beveridge, Albert J. Abraham Lincoln, 1809–58. 2 vols. New York, 1928.

Carey, Charles H. History of Oregon. Portland, 1922.

Clark, Robert Carlton. History of the Willamette Valley Oregon. Chicago, 1927.

Cleland, Robert Glass. California in Our Time 1900–1940. New York, 1947.

Hibbard, Benjamin Horace. A History of the Public Land Policies. New York, 1924.

Nevins, Allan. Ordeal of the Union. 2 vols. New York, 1947.

Quiett, Glenn Chesney. They Built the West: An Epic of Rails and Cities. New York, 1934.

Robbins, Roy Marvin. Our Landed Heritage. Princeton, 1942.

Teele, Ray P. The Economics of Land Reclamation in the United States. New York, 1927.

Treat, Payson J. The National Land System 1785–1820. New York, 1910.

Turner, Frederick Jackson. The United States 1830–50: The Nation and Its Sections. New York, 1935.

Winther, O. O. The Great Northwest. New York, 1947.

THE DEVELOPMENT OF PUBLIC LAND IN THE UNITED STATES

An Arno Press Collection

Bartley, Ernest R. **The Tidelands Oil Controversy.** 1953

Bayard, Charles J. **The Development of the Public Land Policy, 1783-1820, With Special Reference to Indiana** (Doctoral Dissertation, Indiana University, 1956). 1979

Bledsoe, S[amuel] T[homas]. **Indian Land Laws.** 1909

Copp, Henry N[orris]. **Manual for the Use of Prospectors on the Mineral Lands of the United States.** 1897

Copp, Henry N[orris]. **Public Land Laws.** 1875

Copp, Henry N[orris]. **United States Mineral Lands.** 1882

Dana, Samuel Trask and Myron Krueger. **California Lands.** 1958

Davison, Stanley R. **The Leadership of the Reclamation Movement, 1875-1902** (Doctoral Dissertation, University of California, Berkeley, 1952). 1979

Gould, Clarence P. **The Land System in Maryland, 1720-1765.** 1913

Ise, John. **Our National Park Policy.** 1961

Johnson, V. Webster and Raleigh Barlowe. **Land Problems and Policies.** 1954

Martz, Clyde O. **Cases and Materials on the Law of Natural Resources.** 1951

Malone, Joseph J. **Pine Trees and Politics.** 1964

Montgomery, Mary and Marion Clawson. **History of Legislation and Policy Formation of the Central Valley Project.** 1946

O'Callaghan, Jerry A. **The Disposition of the Public Domain in Oregon.** 1960

Peters, William E. **Ohio Lands and Their History.** 1930

Rae, John B. **The Development of Railway Land Subsidy Policy in the United States** (Doctoral Dissertation, Brown University, 1936). 1979

Shambaugh, Benjamin F[ranklin]. **Constitution and Records of the Claim Association of Johnson County, Iowa.** 1894

Smathers, George H. **The History of Land Titles in Western North Carolina.** 1938

Stewart, Lowell O. **Public Land Surveys.** 1935

Tatter, Henry W. **The Preferential Treatment of the Actual Settler in the Primary Disposition of the Vacant Lands in the United States** (Doctoral Dissertation, Northwestern University, 1933). 1979

Taylor, Paul S. **Essays on Land, Water, and the Law in California.** 1979

U.S. House of Representatives. **The Existing Laws of the United States of a General and Permanent Character, and Relating to the Survey and Disposition of the Public Domain, December 1, 1880.** 1884

U.S. House of Representatives. **Laws of the United States:** Of a Temporary Character, and Exhibiting the Entire Legislation of Congress Upon Which the Public Land Titles Have Depended. Two vols. 1881

U.S. Senate. **A National Plan for American Forestry.** Two vols. 1933

U.S. Senate. **The Western Range.** 1936

Wiel, Samuel C. **Water Rights in the Western States.** Two vols. 1911

Winter, Charles E. **Four Hundred Million Acres.** 1932

Wirth, Fremont P. **The Discovery and Exploitation of the Minnesota Iron Lands.** 1937